Tales Of The Warrior-judges

[illegible]

TALES

OF THE

WARRIOR-JUDGES:

A SUNDAY BOOK FOR BOYS,

BY

J. R. MACDUFF, D.D.,

AUTHOR OF "MEMORIES OF GENNESARET," "MORNING AND NIGHT WATCHES," ETC.

" Other portions of Scripture may be more profitable for doctrine, for correction, for reproof, for instruction in righteousness; but for merely human interest—for the lively touches of ancient manners—for the succession of romantic incidents—for the consciousness that we are living face to face with the persons described—for the tragical pathos of events and characters—there is nothing like the history of the Judges."—Stanley's *Lectures on the Jewish Church*, vol. i., p. 283.

NEW YORK:

ROBERT CARTER & BROTHERS, 530, BROADWAY.

MDCCCLXXIII.

PREFACE.

It has long been my ambition to write a book, or, perhaps, a series of books, for boys, suitable for Sunday reading, which might have the effect of interesting them in some of the more attractive scenes and incidents of Bible history. This purpose I have endeavoured partially, at least, to fulfil in the following pages; and I shall cherish the hope, that the present volume may prove only the commencement of another of the many Juvenile Library Shelves to which youthful hands not unwillingly resort on Sunday afternoons.

The "Tales of the Warrior-Judges" will probably be followed by "The Tales of the Warrior-Kings."

CONTENTS.

I.

STORY OF EHUD.

BOOKS of adventure—the record of brave and heroic exploits—have always had, and must always have, for young minds, a special charm.

The Bible—the Book of books—the oldest of all the world's histories, has its stirring tales too: stories of valour and romantic incident, which have never been surpassed, and which require no fictitious aids or colouring to invest them with abiding interest. From this ample material I am now going to make selection for the pages which follow. Moreover, if the Scriptures have often been likened to a picture-gallery, the Book of Judges may well be called the Hall, or corridor, which contains the battle-pieces of the Sacred Volume—the delineations of the war-age of the old Hebrew nation. In surveying the treasures of that ancient gallery, I shall endeavour, to the best of my ability, to act as guide and interpreter.

I begin with the tale of EHUD, not only because we may consider him as the earliest of the Warrior-Judges, but because, too, his story is less familiar; although it must be owned at the outset, that it possesses by no means the varied interest and incident of the others, nor, in its few details, does it commend itself, as they for the most part do, to our sympathy and admiration.

It takes us in thought, to the site at least, of the city of Jericho. You know that that old Canaanitish town, "fenced up to heaven," had been burnt and destroyed by Joshua, its walls levelled with the ground, and a curse uttered against any one who should attempt to rebuild it. It would appear, however, to have been partially, or, I should rather say, considerably restored, a hundred years afterwards, at which time the incidents I am now to relate took place. Although at this day it is a mere handful of ruins and hovels in the midst of a blasted plain, we can well understand its greatness, importance, and beauty in the earlier period of its history, when surrounded with a huge palm forest, eight miles in length and two in breadth,—its present jungle covered with fields of corn, and gardens containing balsam, olive, vine, fig, palm, and pomegranate trees. In addition to the "border river" at its eastern extremity, this vast plain was watered by other streams, specially by that well-known one flowing from the present Wady Kelt—a deep rocky gorge—"the Valley of Achor"—which all travellers agree in considering the wildest and most picturesque of the glens of south Palestine. Joshua saw at a glance that this City of Palms, which has well been called the "capital of the Jordan Valley," was the key to the new conquest; and although, at the time of which I now write, its real grandeur as a city was gone, I cannot wonder that it was still regarded as a tempting prize for the border tribes on the other side of the Jordan.

King Eglon was at this time monarch of Moab,—the rich, though hilly country stretching from the eastern shores of the Dead Sea to the mountains of Gilead, and whose rocky frontier, overhanging the former, constitutes so conspicuous an object in the view from all the higher parts of Palestine. It was the nation of Moab, you will remember, which, sixty years before, made the determined effort to resist the final approach of Israel to their land of promise, and whose then reigning king endeavoured in vain to bribe the eastern soothsayer, Balaam, to curse Israel. It was the country which afterwards had so interesting a connection with Ruth and David, and whose most recent interest to Bible students is in its relation to the now well-known "Moabite Stone," with its strangely chiselled story of these warrior ages.

Eglon formed a confederacy of the western tribes, assisted by his two neighbours, Ammon and "wild Amalek." He crossed Jordan with his troops, marched through the dense palm forest, and took possession either of the rebuilt fortress of Jericho, or of a new city of palm trees erected on some adjoining site. There could not, I think, have been much of the hero about the Moabite king, for Josephus confirms the account in the Bible, that he was so fat and unwieldy as to be ill suited for taking any part in the art of war. It has often been remarked that he stands alone in Scripture with this distinguishing epithet applied to him. As it is wiry, agile, supple forms which are most familiar to travellers in those Eastern regions, perhaps it was an equally rare characteristic in those days to have a corpulent chief.

However, this giant from the "giant cities" of

the desert—a descendant of the old race of the Rephaim, made a successful attack on the fenced city of the plains. His troops were quartered in it, probably a strong military force. With part of his army he retained possession of the fords of the Jordan, evidently to prevent the tribes of Israel, who had territory on the other side of the river, from crossing it: for had these latter joined their brother Benjamites, they might have materially endangered the position and safety of the foreign usurper. Eglon built for himself, within the walls of the new town, a summer palace, or pavilion. Leaving his own highland home and capital in Moab, he seems to have resided in this, at all events for a considerable part of the season, and that, too, for the space of eighteen years. During that long period he exacted tribute from the new settlers, and especially from the tribe of Benjamin. They would probably be required to bring him so much in money, (in specie,) and so much in cattle and corn, wine and oil.

We need hardly wonder that the Israelites surrendered with a grudge to this heathen king the fruits of their labour and toil. Like all old-world tyrants, he would take every means to exhibit and enforce the "insolence of power." Josephus tells us "he omitted no method whereby he might distress them." They would also, doubtless, dislike much to see one who was a stranger occupying the very Eden of Palestine. His presence alone must have been a constant source of annoyance, harassment, and insult.

But how could they manage to break the yoke, conquer the invader, and recover the luxuriant territory? They had not, so far as they themselves were concerned, much cause for hope. Ever since Joshua's death they had fallen away from the worship of the true God, and had given themselves over to idolatry. The stories we are now to tell of the Warrior-Judges, (indeed of the whole thirteen Judges, warlike and peaceful,) are in Scripture ushered in with the words, "The children of Israel did evil in the sight of the Lord." The God they had thus dishonoured left them very much to the fruit of their own ways. The land was in a state of disorder. They had no king, no head, no chiefs or leaders to rely upon in the hour of danger. By reason, partly of their own apathy and indolence, partly also on account of intermarriage with the people of the land, they had failed to do Jehovah's bidding to the extent they might have done, by driving out the old race of Canaanites. A writer justly observes, that "the Hebrews formed little else than an army of occupation in Palestine. Scarcely can we point to a district of the country of which they had exclusive possession. In the Sacred narratives we find the ancient inhabitants in the south and in the north, in the east and in the west: they fill the plains, they occupy the hills, in the valleys they lie in ambush, and from not a few of the strongholds they defy the bold invader," (*Library of Bib. Lit.*, vol. V.) Some of these warlike hordes retained the central fortress of Jebus, on the rocky steeps of Zion. The Philistines and others held the fertile strips of territory on the sea coast, and the fortified cities of Megiddo and Bethshan, on the great plain of Esdraelon. And now this giant from the giant stock of Moab had stolen, for long years, the fairest jewel from the crown of the conquerors,—the same territory which had dazzled the covetous eye of Lot, when he looked down upon it, five hundred years before, from the uplands of Bethel, and regarded it (well he might do so) "as the garden of the Lord, like the land of Egypt," (Gen. xiii. 10.)

I can imagine that these dispirited, evil-doing Israelites, having lost faith in God and faith in themselves, would almost abandon hope of wresting the fair fields and dwellings of Jericho from this Goliath of the East. Many would, I daresay, make up their minds to continue in a state of helpless vassalage, bringing yearly to its gates their hard-earned money, and the flocks and herds, the corn and fruits required to feed their own families. It was the submission of despair.

Although we know, on too good authority, of the widespread corruption among them of which I have spoken, yet their historian tells us too, that "God was moved to compassion by their supplications put up to Him." We may therefore hope and believe that, in the midst of the general disorder and degeneracy, there were a few faithful, loyal hearts—like the future 7000 in Elijah's time, who did not cease to utter the old wilderness prayer, "Arise, O Lord, and let thine enemies be scattered." Indeed we have the express words at the beginning of the story in the Book of Judges—"The children of Israel cried unto the Lord," (Judges iii. 15.)

And how was the cry and prayer of the faithful remnant answered, and the palm-tree Capital made once more their own?

As has generally been the case in all great and successful efforts at freedom, the blow was struck by one brave hand. It is a strange and wild story of a wild time; and though we cannot admire the deceit which the hero of it practised, yet we must do honour at all events to his bravery. We cannot say that the means justified the end, still, the end was a great and important one. His name, though not mentioned along with others in the future warrior songs and psalms of the Hebrews, would doubtless be held in grateful remembrance by the tribes his boldness and valour had delivered from the oppressor's yoke.

This hero—a Benjamite—was apparently a youth, by name Ehud. We are bound to fancy him a very different person in appearance from his royal enemy: muscular, wiry, and nimble like a gazelle on the mountains. Josephus speaks of him as "a man of a very strong body, fit for hard labour, but best skilled in using his left hand, in which was his whole strength." Indeed, this left-hand power seems strangely enough to have belonged to his tribe; for the same writer, in describing a great pitched battle, some years before, between the Benjamites and the other Israelites, specially mentions that "five hundred of the archers slung stones with their left hand." We read, in a subsequent chapter in Judges, of a still greater number of the same tribe, who, as slingers, had this peculiarity; and so perfect, moreover, were they in the warlike art, as to be able to project stones at a hair and not miss it, (xx. 16.) This is all the more remarkable as "Benjamin" signifies "the son of the *right* hand." Alike in soul and body, in heroic bravery and physical strength, Ehud seems to have been well suited for his desperate enterprise.

We shall describe what may be called his 'tactics.' He would appear to have been residing, for the time at all events, in Jericho. And as Orientals are always gratified by receiving presents, even from those who are far below them in station,—the artful Benjamite, according to the account given by Josephus, began his scheme, (which was nothing short of plotting the death of the King of Moab,) by carrying, personally, gifts of various kinds from himself and his tribe to the summer palace; thus insinuating himself into the good graces not only of Eglon, but of his courtiers and royal servants. It is more than probable that he may also have been selected as deputy or representative, to convey the yearly tribute from the tribe, of which I have already spoken. Be this as it may, he seems, at all events, to have successfully masked his true character and design. The king may have admired the intelligence and courage of the wily young Israelite, and, without suspicion, have admitted him to his confidence.

"From the description we have of the manner in

which this tribute was on one occasion presented, the various matters of which it was composed appear to have been borne by a great number of persons, who, marching in orderly procession, successively laid down their valuable burdens before the king. This is in perfect conformity with modern Eastern manners. Tributes, the products of provinces, the gifts periodically or occasionally tendered to a sovereign, are always presented in great state, and with much solicitude, to enhance the apparent extent of the offering. Four or five men or horses are laden with what might most easily be carried by one; and jewels, trinkets, and other articles of value, which one tray might very well hold, are displayed in ten or fifteen. So it was also in ancient times, as we find by the sculptures of Persia and the paintings of Egypt, in which interesting exhibitions of such processions of tribute-bearers are to be found," (Dr. Kitto's *Bible Illustrations*, vol. II., p. 331.) Such a prolonged and pompous ceremonial leads us to understand the meaning of the expression in the Sacred narrative, that he "*had made an end*" in the offering of the tribute, (iii. 18.)

Let us imagine, then, Ehud heading this pageant of tribute-bearers of the tribe of Benjamin. In the meanwhile he had fashioned for himself a dagger with two edges. This he hid by keeping it close to his right thigh, under the folds of the long robe, or abbây,—the same kind of dress which still may be seen, in tattered shape, on the person of the sheikh of the savage villagers who tenant the huts of modern Jericho. He and his imposing train presented themselves before the king. But while delivering the present, Ehud artfully scanned the localities of the palace and audience chamber, in order to discover the safest and surest way, on a second visit, of accomplishing the daring feat. He does not seem, in the meanwhile, to have deemed it necessary to inform his attendants as to what his own secret purpose was. Dismissing them, on the delivery of the present, at the palace door or city gate, he himself pursued his way, alone, by the outskirts of the palm forest at Gilgal, to a spot called in the Bible account "the Quarries."* There has been a considerable diversity of opinion as to what may be signified by this word. Dr. Kitto, whose Biblical research is always interesting and reliable, derives it from a word which signifies to "cut" or "carve;" and he imagines the reference may be to some graven images that had been carved and set up in this place by the invading Moabites: more-

* "The quarries that were by Gilgal," (Judg. iii. 19.)

over, that as it was here, after crossing Jordan, the Hebrew tribes set up their twelve memorial stones taken out of the bed of the river, these images of heathen deities may have been purposely erected to profane one of the "holy places" of the Israelites, (just as the Ark, in a future year, was profaned by being sent to the Temple of Dagon.) It is an exceedingly probable conjecture of this able writer, that one of the most hallowed spots in Israel's memory was thus desecrated and profaned by the idols of the conquerors,—possibly each stone converted into a pedestal for these graven images. If so, it would be an additional evidence as to every means having been employed by the haughty foe to humble and exasperate the subject race. Doubtless Ehud's present visit, by disclosing the sacrilege that had been committed on a consecrated place, would nerve his arm for the accomplishment of his desperate deed. This interpretation of the expression "the Quarries" does not, moreover, exclude a kindred surmise—that some religious feeling may have mingled with his motive in repairing to the old scene of Israel's encampment. Being far distant from Shiloh, (the recognised sanctuary, where the Ark now was,) he may have regarded Gilgal in the light of a subordinate oracle or shrine. Along with other associations, may it not possibly have been the spot ever afterwards deemed sacred, at, or nigh which, Joshua had seen the Captain of the Lord's host with the sword drawn in his hand, and which was pronounced by that mysterious Personage to be holy ground? Stained as Ehud's hands were soon to be with blood, he may have wished thus to invest his act with a religious sanction. He had got the repute in his tribe of being an inspired man—gifted with more than human power. Perhaps his resort to such a sanctuary would alike imbue himself with new resolution, and, if his scheme were successful, demonstrate to the nation that he had been raised up by the God of Israel as an instrument for the deliverance of His oppressed people.

In the simple and brief account contained in the Book of Judges—he "turned himself again from the Quarries," and hastened once more to the fortress. He is soon standing in the presence of the king. If the twofold supposition regarding the grove at Gilgal be correct, he would be able to tell his unsuspecting victim that he had just been at the place recognised as "holy" by the religious rites both of Moabites and Israelites; and that as a prophet of God, he had come to disclose to him a dream or vision he had there received. The corpulent monarch was sitting in a "summer parlour, which he had for himself alone," (Judges iii. 20,) a word rendered in the margin "parlour of cooling." These special chambers were situated then—as in many Eastern dwellings of considerable size still—either in the lower gardens adjoining the house, with refreshing fountains rising in the midst of aquatic plants; or, more frequently, in the upper and highest part of the building, corresponding with the modern word *Belvidere;* only, unlike the latter, in not being entirely open, without roof or canopy. A portion, at all events was formed of elaborate lattice work, so constructed as to exclude the sun, and yet to admit the air, and whatever grateful breezes the climate and situation would allow. If we further employ another modern term, "Conservatory," it would enable us to add an additional idea to the true conception of this "parlour of cooling;" for it would be beautified with tropical plants and creepers—resembling a gigantic bower covered and festooned with nature's own green awning of gourd and palm, honeysuckle and aromatic plant,—an "arbour," on a large scale, similar to that of the prophet of Nineveh. On a raised platform, (or *divan,*) in the upper end of such a *chiosk*, would be seated the portly king of Moab.

Those only who have been in the Jordan valley

and plain of Jericho—the torrid zone of Palestine—can imagine what a relief it would be at that hot season, when the whole atmosphere seems palpitating, for one with an unwieldy "habit of body" to take refuge from the sultry heat of the lower chambers of the pavilion, and obtain what little air could be had in an artificial "summer-house." Not only was the season summer, but Josephus further notes, that the dexterous assassin purposely selected the middle of the day, when the main body-guard of the king had gone to their noontide rest or meal, and when he would have least chance of being interrupted in the bloody tragedy. The bearer of gifts a few hours before, a second time announces to the unwary monarch, that he has a Divine revelation to communicate,—"I have a message from God unto thee," (v. 20.)

So frequent was assassination among these Eastern tribes, that the utmost circumspection was used in admitting any one to the presence of royalty. Very possibly the members of Eglon's body-guard would carefully scrutinize Ehud, (and all the more so as he was an Israelite,) in case of any sword or dagger being about his person. On the left thigh, however—the most likely place for a weapon to be secreted—there was none; and they would not suspect that such might lurk concealed under the folds of the cloak at the right side. In accordance with Oriental usages, whenever Eglon hears of the sacred character of the message and messenger, he orders the few servants that remained with him —probably the soldiers on watch—to leave the apartment, enjoining them to keep silence. His wishes are immediately obeyed. The audience chamber is cleared, and the bloated king, all unconsciously, is alone in the presence of his murderer.

Ehud sees that his longed-for opportunity is come at last. But yet still he "bides his time." He is resolved, if he can, not only to strike the blow, but to do it so thoroughly, that no noise or struggle may for some hours betray the secret. If the dagger can be made to do its work instantaneously, he might easily elude the vigilance of the guards, and have time to sound the war-cry ere the deed be discovered. He saw, however, the difficulty, owing to the monarch's enormous size, of striking a blow that would be fatal; so long, at all events, as the other retained his sitting posture on his throne. How could he manage to get him to stand upright? His inventiveness is here, too, equal to the occasion. The announcement of the Divine message, which has succeeded so well in clearing the chamber of the body-guard, may be employed with equal success to effect the other. With a far different meaning from the words as used by the great Christian Apostle, "he caught him with guile."

In similar deference to prevailing custom, upon Ehud's repetition of the religious character of his errand, the portly giant rises from his seat. When in the act of doing so, the former seizes the favourable instant. With that powerful left hand of his, the dagger is drawn, quick as lightning, from its lurking-place in the folds of his garment, and with one fierce plunge, not only blade, but haft also, is buried in the monster's carcase. The point of the short sword had reached the heart; and without shriek or groan he fell prone on the floor, and lay weltering in his blood. Ehud finishes the sanguinary deed as deliberately as he began. He calmly shuts the doors of this upper chamber, and locks them behind him. The guards are still fast asleep. The regicide creeps stealthily along the porch, then by the outside stair or gallery which in Eastern houses leads to the court at the basement, and before any trumpet of alarm could be sounded, he is away with fleet foot beyond the possibility of capture. The king's sentinels continue either slumbering, or, what is the same thing, if they have awoke and resumed their watch, they have no suspicion of what has occurred. They listen;—all is still. They imagine that Eglon, having finished his audience with the Israelite, has himself gone to his "siesta," or noontide repose, and they dare not intrude to disturb him. By-and-by, however, their suspicions are roused by the long and unwonted silence. The doors are still locked. The shadows of evening are falling, and no movement in the royal chamber is heard. They evidently first try to make inquiry behind the doors as to the cause; but when there is no reply to their summons, they proceed to effect a forcible entrance. To their horror they see the gigantic corpse of their sovereign stretched on the floor—"their lord was fallen down dead on the earth," (v. 25.)

Meanwhile Ehud had made good his escape. He seems to have gone out of his way, that he might pause again for a moment at "the Quarries" at Gilgal:—(Was this to render thanks at the oracle for the success of his cruel deed?) He resumes, however, his flight, and never takes breath till he has reached the wild mountainous country of Ephraim. He seems to have felt that every moment was of importance. Large cow-horns were used, in these warrior ages, to summon the tribes in the hour of danger, or to prepare for battle. They seem to have resembled the fiery cross in our own northern Highlands, which of yore was employed to muster the clans and retainers when resisting some sudden raid or foray. These rude trumpets were seized by Ehud, and he wakes the echoes of the Ephraim hills with the well understood sound. The rallying notes were speedily answered. In a few hours, a resolute army composed of that powerful tribe, were on march to the Jericho fortress under the young leader; for "they went down from the mount, and he before them," (v. 27.) We are even furnished with his watchword or battle-cry—"Follow after me, for the Lord hath delivered your enemies the Moabites into your hand," (v. 28.) Instead of advancing direct to the city, he had the sagacity to proceed at once to the fords of the Jordan. He saw, at a glance, the desirableness ot seizing hold of this important point—the key of the position,—for through it the panic-stricken troops would be certain to attempt to pass.

A monarch's violent death, in these times, seemed invariably to have the effect of striking terror among his soldiers and people. It was so in the case of Eglon. No sooner was the assassination discovered, than dismay and disorder spread from the palace to the city, and from street to street. The barracks contained "men of valour" (v. 29) to the number of ten thousand. But these troops of the king were the first to flee from the death-stricken fortress, with the design of retreating across the passage of Jordan to their own territory in Moab. Ehud and his brave band, however, were before them, prepared to intercept their march. A brief sanguinary struggle took place; but the demoralized army of Eglon had no chance with the smaller but compact and heroic troop of the Israelite chieftain, who had fired them with his own enthusiasm. The stream of the river was crimsoned with blood:—some perished in the waters, others, who attempted to evade pursuit, were cut down as they attempted to fly. Perhaps in their case this was not so easy, for the Bible narrative speaks of them as "lusty;" a word which in other places means "fat;" and would imply that the king's troops were unwieldy as himself,—equally ill-fitted for a hasty retreat. The corpses of the Moabites lay thick strewn among the reeds and oleanders. Josephus tells us that "not so much as one of them escaped."

We are informed nothing of Ehud's triumphant return to the now deserted fortress, nor as to whether the matrons and maidens, belonging to the liberated tribes of Gad and Benjamin and Judah, came out, as in a future age, with songs and dances to greet the victor. Doubtless his name would be enrolled among the greater warriors of the nation; and their historian tells us, that for a long period he continued to govern the people whom he had so bravely rescued from servitude. There were no more forays made by the fierce Arabs of Moab, Ammon, or Amalek, for nearly a century. The blessings of peace were happily secured—"the land had rest fourscore years," (v. 31.) A writer mentions, what may be worthy of note in passing, that a trace of this invasion of Moab is visible in the name of one of the towns of Benjamin, which is called Cephar-ha-Ammonai—the "hamlet of the Ammonites," (Smith's *Bible Dictionary*, *Art.* "*Moab.*")

I may make the same observation, in closing this story, regarding Ehud, (which may be repeated in regard to other warrior-chiefs whose exploits we have still to relate,) that while, as Christians, we must regard with horror their barbarities and cruelties—their tortuous ways—their treachery and deceit,—yet we must judge of him and them by another standard from that by which we judge those of our own age. They lived in a dark and corrupt period;—even the light of truth which Israel had enjoyed in a previous century, was sadly dimmed. No great prophet had, for a long time, been raised up to teach them alike their duty to Jehovah and to one another. They had got so accustomed to war and cruelty—to cunning and artifice—to crime and revenge, that these had become a second nature to them. If we condemn them, let us first rather condemn ourselves for our many sins against God and our fellows, with all our superior advantages. Their age corresponded with the first part of the prophet Elijah's vision on Horeb—when he saw the wind, and the earthquake, and the fire, breaking the mountains and rending the rocks. They had not heard, as we have, the still small voice of Gospel love and peace and forgiveness.

And yet, though the Bible narrative be silent, may we not hope better things even of Ehud and his warrior tribe? Who knows but when a grateful people came, once more, to settle down among the palm and acacia groves and gardens of Jericho—each one sitting under his vine and fig tree, with no Moabite invader to make them afraid,—that they would be led to remember a greater Deliverer than their brave leader;—even Him, whose twofold name was, "the Lord of Hosts," "the God of Israel."*

* May we not possibly draw this inference from Judges iv. 1?

There was no Temple as yet reared, like that which was built in Jerusalem afterwards, whither the tribes might "go up." The sanctuaries of Bethel and Shiloh were at a distance. But who can tell whether the new dwellers in the plain and city of Jericho—after having overthrown the hideous idols of Moab which so long desecrated the old entrance-gate to the promised land—may not have loved from time to time to congregate, as devout worshippers, at the little oracle by the banks of the Jordan, and there sing some such song as that we are to speak of in our next—"They that are delivered from the noise of archers in the places of drawing water: there shall they rehearse the righteous acts of the Lord, even the righteous acts towards the inhabitants of His villages in Israel," (Judges v. 11.)

II.

STORY OF DEBORAH.

THE Warrior-Judge who is to form the heroine of our second story, is DEBORAH. She may well be included in these Tales, and her name placed on the roll of Israel's champions; for not only is she expressly spoken of as "judging Israel,"—"the children of Israel came up to her for judgment," (Judges iv. 4, 5,)—but she bears, also, not the least prominent and chivalrous part in one of the most decisive campaigns of Hebrew history, or indeed of any age.

Ehud and his generation were by this time sleeping in their graves. Ammon, and Moab, and Amalek had not again dared to molest the inhabitants of South and East Palestine. But a strong and formidable nation had for long held sway in the north, under Jabin; the successor of the same Canaanitish king who had fought against Joshua 150 years before, and whose capital, Hazor, situated on the shores of Lake Merom, had at the same time been destroyed by the commander of Israel. It had now, however, been rebuilt, and Jabin and his tribe had become, what would be called in modern language, a great military power. Artillery and cannon are often spoken of as the "right arm" of modern warfare. In those olden days, before science had invented her fearful powers of destruction, the most formidable weapon consisted in iron chariots, armed with scythes, capable of holding from twenty to fifty men, and which operated with terrible effect, especially in every battle fought in the plains. Palestine, however, is a country which consists more of hills than level ground. The interior, generally speaking, is made up of an endless succession of mountain, and glen, and valley. But near the centre of the country, or rather tending toward the northern extremity, there is one remarkable exception,—the enormous plain of Esdraelon, which traverses the whole extent from Carmel in the west to Jezreel in the east. The clouds of war were at present fast gathering. King Jabin, and his great general, Sisera, knew well the signal advantage their chariots would have (and they had 900 of them) in this open country. Could they only tempt the tribes of Israel to issue from their mountain strongholds and fortresses, to make Esdraelon their battlefield, victory would be certain. As the sequel, however, will shew, the Canaanites were to be taught that there was a Power above, mightier than the mightiest, and which could make the very stars in their courses to fight against Sisera.

As in the time of Ehud, so was it now; the Israelites were utterly unprepared for an encounter with disciplined troops. The land had never recovered from its anarchy and disorder. Any army they had was little to be depended upon. Indeed it would be a truer description that they had no army at all. As it is expressed in the Sacred narrative, "there was no spear nor shield among forty thousand in Israel." The Canaanites had evidently taken the most effectual means of completing the subjugation by disarming the people,—leaving them without weapons, either for the defence of their homes, or for use in active war. And even if their armoury had been full, they had no brave or patriotic leader to rally them in this their hour of degradation, and wake them up to the memory of former heroic times and heroic deeds. What was worse—the great

"King of Jeshurun"—the true God their fathers worshipped, was renounced and disowned: for, once more is the narrative of the new war ushered in by the words, "And the children of Israel again did evil in the sight of the Lord," (Judges iv. 1.)

What was to be done? They were now, and had been for twenty years, under cruel servitude to this northern tyrant. His yoke of bondage seemed, like his chariots, to be of iron. The words of the Sacred story are short, but explicit, "He mightily oppressed them," (Judges iv. 3.) They had a far more formidable king to subdue, and a far more formidable fortress to raze, than that of Jericho. But where or whence are they to look for deliverance or a deliverer? What Ehud is there to sound the war notes, and, alike by desperate courage and promptitude in action, to gather the faint-hearted tribes, that they may free themselves from a thraldom which is becoming yearly more intolerable?

I must take you again in thought to that wild mountainous region in the middle of Palestine, where we found, in our last story, the young Benjamite blowing his trumpet, and mustering the warrior Ephraimites to battle.

Somewhere near Bethel, where Abraham built his altar, and Jacob dreamed his dream, there dwelt a remarkable woman. Her name was Deborah, a word which Josephus reminds us, means in Hebrew "Bee;" and as the bee was the Egyptian symbol of kingly power, some have thought it was given her to denote the regal influence she was to exercise over her countrymen. Dr. Kitto remarks, that her's forms "one of a class of names such as are derived from material objects, not uncommon in Scripture. Thus we find Rachel, a lamb; Chasidah, a stork; Hadessah, (Esther,) a myrtle; Tamar, a palm tree; Caleb, a dog; Nehushta, a serpent; Irad, a wild ass; Achbar, a mouse; Agabus, a locust; Cephas, a rock or stone; and many others. Nor are such names unknown to us. Thus we have Margaret, a pearl; Agnes, a lamb; Phillis, a green bough; Penelope, a species of bird; Giles, a little goat; Lionel, a little lion, &c." Deborah was evidently a woman of great moral courage, a true heroine,—the Boadicea, the Joan of Arc of her time. Not only so, but she was Poetess, and Prophetess, and Judge in one. The inspired song we shall afterwards find her singing, is allowed to be one of the grandest ever written. A well-known historian of the Jews, himself no mean poet, says of it—"Lyric poetry has nothing in any language which can surpass the boldness and animation of this striking production," (Milman's *History of the Jews*, vol. I., p. 246.)

Such was the deliverer divinely raised up at this momentous and critical period of the nation's history. However apostate her other countrymen were from the faith of their fathers, her hymn of victory tells us she was "strong in faith, giving glory to God." Had she lived in the times of the future Psalmist of the nation, she would have sung with him, "Some trust in chariots, and some in horses; but we will remember the name of the Lord our God," (Psalm xx. 7.)

The trees of Palestine often gave names to particular places. Jericho, as we have seen, was called "the city of palms;" Bethany signifies "the house of dates;" plantations or groves of olives gave name to the well-known "mount which is before Jerusalem." Solitary spots, too, were distinguished in the same way:—as, Abraham's oak at Mamre; or the oak tree at Bethel which marked the grave of Rebekah's nurse, and which received the name of "the oak of weeping." Deborah's seat of judgment was under some similarly noted palm on Mount Ephraim. This species of tree was found in Palestine only on the lower levels, such as in the plains of Jericho or Gennesaret. The palm tree under which our heroine dwelt, would probably, therefore, be a remarkable exception among the trees which clothed the mountains of her tribe. It may have been invested on that account with a sort of sacredness by the people around—regarded, perhaps, like the cedar of Lebanon, as "the tree of God." This particular tree has been supposed to be the same which is spoken of in connection with another gathering of the children of Israel described in Judges xx. 33, and called "Baal-tamar," which means "the sanctuary of the palm," (Stanley's *Sinai and Palestine*, p. 143.) As the patriarch Job, you may remember, is represented as going forth to "sit at the gate," amid the respectful silence of the elders, princes, and nobles,—so, under this picturesque and shady covering—this noblest and most graceful of nature's tents—with the bright blue sky of Palestine overhead, sat "the wife of Lapidoth." Some, indeed, question if the word 'Lapidoth' refers to her husband at all, for it may be rendered "lightnings," and may possibly refer rather to her own Divine illumination, her brilliant and flaming career—one of God's "ministers of flaming fire." The conjecture is more probable that, if at one time the wife of Lapidoth, she had now become a widow, and, in that position, was abler to act the independent part that had been as-

When the vessel was reeling and foundering she alone had resolution to seize the helm.

I doubt not she would have had bravery enough to leave her palm tree, and personally to conduct the campaign; but this would have been an eternal disgrace to the *men* of the tribes. Among these, moreover, she had been divinely directed to one, who she knew would be equal to the occasion. She summons him from his home in the far north, and instals him as leader of the armies of Israel. His name (so again are we reminded by Josephus) is similar to what we have seen may possibly have been the meaning of her own—*Barak*, which signifies 'lightning.' He obeys the call. She informs him that his selection for the command is not her's, but that of the God of his fathers. She enjoins him, in Jehovah's name, to gather together 10,000 men from the tribes of Naphtali and Zebulun, and march with them to the great mustering place, or rendezvous, on the top of Mount Tabor; while she at the same time would, by skilful manœuvring, decoy Sisera, the general of King Jabin, towards the river Kishon, and, amidst its swamps and morasses, entangle and destroy his army. Barak is not so bold as his sister heroine. At all events he undertakes the campaign on the one condition, that

Deborah would accompany him to guide their operations in the field. He would probably feel that the moral effect of her person near the scene of conflict, would be of signal importance to his soldiers. It would be to the Israelites an equivalent for all Jabin's chariots of iron. It would tell upon them as the conscious presence of the ark of the covenant did in more than one future battle; and while she rebukes Barak for meanly delivering up his power thus to a woman's hands, and warns him that another than he will have the glory of the fight, she will not allow the issue to be imperilled by her refusal, and we are told, "Deborah arose, and went with Barak to Kedesh," (Judges iv. 9.)

Her song, given in the fifth chapter of Judges, gives a vivid and pictorial account as to how the various tribes of Israel answered to her war-summons. The most of them did so eagerly and with alacrity, a few held timidly aloof. The tribes which had suffered most from Jabin's oppression were, as was to be expected, most eager for the encounter. "Zebulun and Naphtali were a people that jeoparded their lives unto the death in the high places of the field," (v. 18.) The tribes beyond Jordan, being at a long distance from the scene, selfishly refused to leave their cities. The children of Dan, whose possessions were by the sea-shore, had ships to flee to in case of disaster: Jabin's iron chariots could not reach them there; and selfishness in their case also gained the day. The same with Asher—he could retreat to the precipitous rocks which guarded his maritime border, or busy himself with his fishing and merchandise. The pastoral tribe of Reuben resolved to keep by their herds and sheepfolds. This was not a unanimous decision: some brave men in the tribe were evidently ready to exchange the bleatings of the flocks for the din of the martial camp. There was a keen debate on the question: some on the side of high-souled patriotism and duty, some for selfish ease and inactivity:—"For the divisions of Reuben there were great searchings of heart." Deborah's own tribe, the powerful and warlike one of Ephraim, naturally responded with its wonted enthusiasm to the summons of its own heroine; and Benjamin, now, as at other times, was their confederate—"after thee, Benjamin," (v. 14.) Issachar may possibly have at first been among the lukewarm and apathetic. But Deborah's presence, as she passed through the tribe, riding on her white ass, (v. 10,) and singing her war song, "My heart is toward the governors of Israel, that offer themselves willingly among the people," (v. 9,) decided the waverers—"the princes of Issachar were with Deborah," (v. 15.) And if she had been successful in raising the patriot spirit, she is not forgetful to give the glory to whom it is due:—"The Lord made me have dominion over the mighty," (v. 13.)*

Such, then, is the muster of Israel, in all 10,000 men. The tribes of Judah and Simeon alone have no mention made of them. It has been surmised that they may have been engaged in suppressing one of the frequent forays of the turbulent Philistines, although it is as likely that some jealous feeling of the other rival neighbours may have been the cause of their absence. Despite of the widespread anarchy, disorder, and indifference, the general laxity in social virtues and martial discipline, of which I have spoken, it must nevertheless be owned, from what we have now said, that Deborah's chivalrous appeal was followed by a noble outburst of heroic patriotism. It shews, indeed, that these qualities were not extinct, but only slumbering. It only required some one of true, devoted spirit, like this Judge and Prophetess, to apply the torch in order to set the land in conflagration. When she came

* See the gathering of the tribes well described in Dr. Stanley's *Lectures*, vol. I., p. 320.

afterwards to write or to sing her song of victory, she is proud to own the heartiness with which the tribes responded at last to her martial summons. "The people willingly offered themselves," (v. 2;) "the governors (the chiefs) offered themselves willingly among the people," (v. 9.) She feels the troops deserve well to be called "the mighty," (v. 13.)

But to proceed with the story. I have already mentioned that there was a peculiarly favourable place for the massing of all these various tribal soldiers on Mount Tabor. This is a mountain of a singular conical shape, covered with profuse vegetation, which rises conspicuous to the north of the plain of Esdraelon. It is one of the most picturesque spots in Palestine; and, in addition to its association with many events in Old Testament story, it is surrounded with places, (some of them visible from its summit,) which were yet to receive their most sacred interest in future centuries—not from warrior kings, but from the life and ministry of the Divine "Prince of peace." As Deborah and Barak together then stood in the midst of their troops on its green platform, their eyes would fall to the right on the yet unknown valley and village of Nazareth; Nain nestled on one of the slopes of the great plain in front; while to the left, or rather behind, the hill-tops were visible which enshrined in a deep hollow the lake of Chinneroth, whose shores, under the more familiar name of Tiberias or Gennesaret, were destined to be trodden, even more than Jerusalem itself, by the holy footsteps of the Son of God. These visions of peace were now, however, far distant. Before that era was to dawn upon the world, Tabor had to look down upon many a fierce battle waged in the fields below, of which this imminent one of Megiddo was not the least sanguinary.

Meanwhile, the enormous army of Sisera, who had been apprized of the movements of the vassal tribes by Heber the Kenite, has descended to Megiddo, a fortified town on the south-west corner of the extended plain, watered by the Kishon. Josephus is at times somewhat perplexing in his numbers. It is so in this case; for he mentions Jabin's iron chariots to be 3000, while he swells the amount of fighting men to 300,000 footmen and 10,000 cavalry. These statements, however, of the historian, are nothing to the incredible numbers which, according to Jewish tradition, were assembled under Sisera. The absurd story would assign no less than 40,000 generals to the Canaanite army, with a still more impossible host of soldiers under each. But the height of the wild legend is reached, when Sisera's own war chariot is represented as drawn by 900 horses!* Even making every deduction, alike from the statement of Josephus and the more foolish one of the Jewish chroniclers, it must have been a formidable host which were then gathered on the heights of Tabor. The bravest of the 10,000 must have had their own misgivings about the result of so unequal a conflict; and the most pious among them would have good reason to say, in the words of a future warlike monarch of their own nation, "We have no might against this great company that cometh against us, neither know we what to do; but our eyes are upon thee," (2 Chron. xx. 12.)

The whole army of Sisera must have been seen by the Israelites from the top of Tabor, through an opening in the hills;—the eagle looked down from afar upon its prey;—and Deborah, who herself was in the midst of the troops, saw that everything depended on the swiftness and suddenness of the swoop from the woody eyrie. We might have thought differently;—that it would have been safer for the comparative handful of Israelites to have kept their sure ground on the heights of Tabor, where Jabin's chariots, with their iron blades, could not operate. This, doubtless, would have been the

* Note, Dr. Smith's *Bible Dictionary*, *Art.* "*Sisera.*"

case, had not "the shout" of a Mightier than earthly king been among them. But Deborah had evidently one thought—that of magnifying, alike in the eyes of all Israel and of their enemies, the great name of Jehovah, who could save or conquer "as well by few as by many." "The lofty looks of man shall be humbled, and the haughtiness of men shall be bowed down, and the Lord alone shall be exalted in that day. For the day of the Lord of hosts shall be upon every one that is proud and lofty, and upon every one that is lifted up; and he shall be brought low; and upon all the cedars of Lebanon, that are high and lifted up, and upon all the oaks of Bashan," (Isaiah ii. 11-13.)

There is no time lost. A clear voice—more inspiriting than any trumpet-tone—is heard giving the word of command. It is that of the heroine herself—"Up, Barak; for this is the day in which the Lord hath delivered Sisera into thine hand: is not the Lord gone out before thee?" (Judg. iv. 14.)

With this watchword, this assurance from inspired lips of certain victory, the tents are left, and down the slopes of the mountain the ranks of Barak hasten to close with the vast host encamped in the distance. They are all foot soldiers. Sword and spear, bow and sling, and such other weapons of war as they had managed to secrete, (notwithstanding the disarmament of which I have spoken,)—are all they have to match the horses and war chariots of the Canaanites. It must have been, too, in the first instance, a long and fatiguing march of twelve miles before they could close with the enemy. Nor was this all. The plain of Esdraelon was doubtless then, as now, covered with rank vegetation—long grass and reeds, bog and morass—that would impede the advance of the soldiers, and give the fresh troops of Sisera a great advantage over them.

But other things were overruled by a Divine hand to counterbalance these evils, and to favour the Israelites, independent altogether of the panic which the boldness and bravery of such an advance would inspire into the hearts of the Canaanites. Deborah, in her after song, tells us, "They fought from heaven; the stars in their courses fought against Sisera," (v. 20.) The clear blue sky—as is often the case in these countries—suddenly grew black with tempest; the clouds gathered; hail and rain descended in torrents; aided by a furious wind from the north-east, the storm fell with all its vengeance on the van of Sisera's army, and blinded the eyes of his soldiers; so much so, that it was impossible to see before them or to use their weapons. Josephus adds, that they were unable even to grasp their sword-hilts by reason of the cold. But added to this—the drenching rain produced more fatal effects still. The river Kishon, rising near Jezreel at the eastern extremity of the great plain, winds its solitary way along, till it falls into the Mediterranean, near the base of Mount Carmel. It is fed by a number of streams from the adjoining hills on either side. Its volume is not large or formidable in ordinary times; but after a sudden rainfall or thunderstorm, when every adjoining rill is rapidly swollen, it becomes a furious eddying torrent, overflowing its banks, and sweeping all before it. It was this "Kishon—that ancient river, the river Kishon," which decided the fortunes of that memorable day. Far more fatal and formidable than all the slings, and stones, and arrows of Israel, were these watery arrows from the bow of heaven. For soon the plain became an impassable morass. The iron chariots, which would otherwise have swept all before them, were rendered useless. The wheels stuck in the mud. The horses reared and plunged, sinking to the fetlocks in the soft mire. "Then were the horse-hoofs broken by means of the prancings, the prancings of their mighty ones," (v. 22.) The war steeds then, like the Arab horses to this day, were never shod; so that their hoofs were broken in the violent effort to extricate themselves. Even those that succeeded in getting disentangled, were thus unable, by reason of their mangled and shattered hoofs, to bear along the heavy chariots, and the disabled charioteers were made an easy prey to the swords and bowmen of Israel.

The confusion increased—horses, chariots, and charioteers were equally helpless. The rest of the army, seized with panic, attempted in vain to flee. They had the unsparing Israelites on one side, and the impetuous river on the other. The latter swept thousands down in its whirling eddies. It was a repetition of the old scene of Pharaoh and his host, with the drowning horse and its rider;—the banks of the Kishon, like the shores of the Red Sea, were strewn with dead and dying. Nor, though it was on a smaller scale, may it be out of place to note the repetition in more modern times of a similar disaster. For we are told that after the battle of Tabor, when the Turkish troops, in the same place, retreated before the victorious army of Napoleon, they underwent a like fate in their attempt to cross the treacherous flood.

Doubtless Deborah's battle-cry would still be

ringing in the ears of Barak and his men—"Up! is not the Lord gone out before thee?" The compact mass of Israelites, unencumbered with chariots or baggage, pushed after the retreating army. The rout was complete, and the slaughter terrible. It would have been more so still—there would not have been a single Canaanite left to tell the tale—had it not been for the "criminal inactivity" of one adjacent town—that of Meroz. Its citizens shut their gates, and refused to join their brethren in the pursuit. Deborah did not forget their unworthy and unpatriotic conduct. She branded the name with infamy, for all future ages, in her song. She speaks as if she had Divine authority in uttering her malison:—"Curse ye Meroz, said the angel of the Lord, curse ye bitterly the inhabitants thereof; because they came not to the help of the Lord, to the help of the Lord against the mighty," (v. 23.) There is no such place now to be found nigh the Kishon; probably the curse was fully carried out, and every stone of the denounced city overthrown and destroyed. It is conjectured, however, that it may have commanded the pass near Jezreel, by which the fugitive army must have retreated; so that, if they had done their duty, by making common cause with their brethren, none could have escaped.

There is a curious Jewish tradition indeed, that Meroz, (which signifies "secret,") was not a town at all, but the troop of evil angels which led on the Canaanites; and that the angel who, in Deborah's song, instigates the curse, is Michael, the angel of Jehovah, the leader of the Israelites.*

The interest of the story now centres on the Canaanitish leader. Sisera partakes in the horrible panic and ignominious retreat. Though rejecting the absurd Jewish legend, we may believe his chariot would doubtless be conspicuous among the rest, for its size, and strength, and workmanship; and in it would be harnessed the fleetest chargers. But in vain can it save him now. By remaining there he would only attract the enemies' notice, and become a certain mark for their slings and arrows. He therefore vaults from it to the ground, casts his weapons away, and flies on foot as best he may, (for it is his only chance of escape,) to seek shelter among the green hills of Galilee.

He possibly would take flight by the very road which was familiar to the blessed Redeemer himself in future days—hastening by Nazareth and the mountains at the north-west of the Lake of Tiberias, till he came down on the pastoral valleys

* See Dr. Smith's *Bible Dictionary*, *Art.* "*Meroz.*"

around Kadesh. Or, another route, more natural for him, was to follow the track of his retreating army, by the eastern end of Esdraelon, (the same direction by which they had approached,) and thus he might have obtained refuge in his own city of Harosheth. There were those, at all events, in that city, who were anxiously looking for him,—expecting every moment to receive tidings, not of defeat, but of certain victory. The mother of Sisera — the "mother queen"—the chieftainess, was standing on the summit of the fortress—perhaps of the hero's own palace or castle — looking wistfully through the embrasures or latticed window. The hours of the day were rapidly advancing;—no messenger had yet been seen coming, with fleet foot, with the longed for intelligence. The high-born, impatient dame chides the delay—"Why is his (triumphal) chariot so long in coming? why tarry the wheels of his chariot?" She has a band of companions—the princesses, and matrons, and damsels, who have sons and brothers in the battle — gathered on these lofty battlements, to share with her in the pride of victory and spoils of war. In answer to the constant demand, "Why is his chariot so long in coming?" she, and they beguile the weary hours of watching, by numbering up the proud trophies that will fall to the conquerors. To each chief, as to Naaman of a future age, there will be one—it may be two captive maids, or female slaves. With the love of adornment so characteristic of Orientals, they have their eyes on the bracelets, and earrings, and nose jewels; the silken cloaks and broidered raiment; the saddle-cloths and rich carpets, that will be numbered among the booty. To Sisera—the great hero of the day—they delight to parcel out, in thought, robes of special beauty in workmanship, glowing with varied colours and rich fringes—"Have they not sped? have they not divided the prey; to every man a damsel or two; to Sisera a prey of divers colours, a prey of divers colours of needlework, of divers colours of needlework on both sides, meet for the necks of them that take the spoil," (Judges v. 30.) Alas! the bright picture is to be changed into sack-cloth and ashes. Ere the sun goes down over Carmel, the terrible truth has been told. A handful of fugitives reach the walls, only to announce that the power of the Canaanites is broken for ever, in this bloody day, by the waters of Megiddo. "There brake He the arrows of the bow, the shield, and the sword, and the battle. The stout-hearted are spoiled, they have slept their sleep; and none of the men of might have found their hands. At thy rebuke, O God of Jacob, both the chariot and horse are cast into a dead sleep," (Psalm lxxvi. 3, 5, 6.)

As the curtain, in this tragic story, here falls on the wild wailings of these disconsolate female mourners at Harosheth, it rises on a very different scene.

It is a green valley, such as I have already alluded to, in the far north of Palestine;—one of the many that cling, with a wild highland beauty, around the roots of Hermon. A strange and unwonted spectacle there meets the eye,—that of a Bedouin encampment. Sheep and goats, camels and asses, are seen cropping the rich pasturage, and roaming at will around some rows of black goats'-hair tents. Two larger tents occupy the centre—shaded by one of those magnificent Terebinths which delight the traveller in Palestine still, from their size and beauty. This must have been a tree specially striking—as it received the name, "the oak of the wanderers," or "the oak of the unloading of tents."* We may further picture in thought a spear stuck in the ground, telling that here is the tent of the chief or

* Judges iv. 11, "mis-translated 'the *plain* of Zaanaim.'" See Stanley's *Sinai and Palestine*, p. 336, note. Also, *Lectures*, p. 324.

sheikh, and beside it that of his wife, or "the harem," —both sacred from intrusion, and especially the latter. It is a settlement of the tribe of Kenites, a section of the family of Jethro, the most faithful friends of Israel in their wanderings in the wilderness. Indeed, they seem to have accompanied the Hebrews through the greater part of the desert, although their encampment was always distinct. On reaching the land of promise, they continued their old love of solitude, and a nomadic life, by avoiding the regular cities and villages, and pitching their tents in the wildernesses of the south. They were descended from Abraham by his wife Keturah, and therefore had pure Hebrew blood in their veins. By some singular accident or caprice, one of their chieftains had wandered thither to the far north of Canaan, and pitched the tents of his tribe amid the olive-clothed mountains and verdant valleys of the most picturesque part of Palestine. What Wales was of old to England, or what Scotland is to her southern sister now, so was that "land of Zabulon and the land of Nephthalim, by the way of the sea, (of Gennesaret,) Galilee of the Gentiles."—(Isaiah ix. 1; Matthew iv. 15.)

A weary, exhausted, blood-stained fugitive is seen with hesitating step approaching. Who could have recognised, in that tattered form, the proud hero who rode out of the streets of Harosheth, three days before, in his war chariot, confident of victory? It is the beaten, humbled leader of the Canaanites. He knows that his own sovereign, Jabin, is on friendly terms with that mountain tribe, and he ventures, in his hour of sore calamity, to claim that *dakheel*, or protection, which an Arab never refuses to an ally. Whether the chief himself (Heber) were absent from the settlement, or no, we cannot tell. It is, at all events, somewhat remarkable that, contrary to all Arab usage and etiquette, Sisera enters the tent, not of the sheikh, but that of the chieftainess. Then, as at this day, as has just been observed, the tent of the women was considered a place alike sacred and inviolable; indeed, the word "*harem*" or "*haram*" signifies "*sacred.*" Doubtless, when the black curtains closed upon the fugitive, he would feel his perfect security. If the troops of avenging Israel were at his heels, and their swords thirsting for his blood, he would feel that he was as safe within that tent as within ramparts of iron: every pursuer knew well the prohibition, "Thus far shalt thou go, and no farther." Sisera, undoubtedly, would not have ventured to claim its shelter had he not received the express sanction and invitation of Jael, the wife of Heber. She had evidently, however, recognised in the distance the faint and famished warrior. She had approached him, and accorded to him at once the unwonted privilege, "Turn in my lord, turn in to me; fear not." On entering, he fell down with fatigue on the floor or divan of the tent; and she threw over his weary limbs a mantle—probably the "*semicah*," one of the divan coverlids. Parched with thirst—perhaps from wounds as well as travel—he prefers the request, "Give me, I pray thee, a little water to drink." Wine would have been the most refreshing beverage in his weary state; but the Kenites—a branch of the Rechabites—were forbidden to taste the juice of the grape. Another and more likely reason may have impelled his petition for a draught of water. He wished to make doubly sure of his security, and of the good faith of his hostess; and receiving a drink of anything from her hands, formed the Arab pledge of honour, friendship, and fidelity. If this cup of hospitality only touch his lips, he can close his weary eyes without one suspicion of treachery. She generously gives him more than he asks. There is abundance of the favourite Arab beverage at hand: pails or distended skins of goat milk are ranged under the shade of the Terebinth.

She opens one of these leathern bottles and pours the contents into "a lordly dish,"—the great bowl, so fashioned at each end as to prevent spilling, which was reserved for occasions of special honour and hospitality. With this milk, supplemented with curd—(or, rather, the sour cream skimmed from the top of an earthen jar,—*leban*, as they call it still,)—the hunger and thirst of the vanquished hero are assuaged, and he would fain lie down and sleep away his fatigue and misery. Before doing so, however, he asks of his protectress a further guarantee of safety. He makes the urgent request, that she will stand in the door of the tent; and, in case of his pursuers tracking him to his "quarry," that she would evade their question, and keep the secret of his concealment, (Judges iv. 20.) Doubly confident, he now composes himself for what he little thought was to be his last long sleep. King Jabin, as I have said, was the ally of this Kenite tribe; but, unknown to Sisera, they were, as has already also been mentioned, the older allies still of Israel. From the lips of Moses himself they had received the seal of perpetual friendship—"What goodness Jehovah shall do unto us, the same will we do to thee," (Numbers x. 32.)

The bold unscrupulous woman—a heroine of a

different stamp from Deborah—resolves to make this previous alliance and blood-relationship the ground and apology for an otherwise enormous crime. Contrary to every principle in the modern code of honour, she resolves to butcher her unsuspecting guest in cold blood. He is now fast asleep. She pulls up one of the nails—one of the wooden pegs which the Arabs use to this day in fastening the tent rope to the ground. With this wooden pin in her left hand, and a workman's hammer, or mallet, in the right,—she stealthily approaches and stands over the slumbering victim. She deliberately selects the uncovered brow for the fatal wound; and then, with one terrible blow, she sends the inglorious weapon through his temples, pinning him down to the earth. "He bowed," we read, "and there fell." We picture one convulsive struggle—one heaving of his breast in wild agony; but it was only momentary; "at her feet he fell; where he bowed, there he fell down dead," (v. 27.) The once proud champion—whose name struck terror into the many thousands of Israel—now lay silent at the feet of a female assassin.

We need not pause in the story to condemn so revolting a breach of sworn fidelity;—in the case too of a defenceless man—the ally of her tribe,—one who had entrusted himself to her keeping, and to whom, in offering the contents of that "lordly dish," she had given what was equivalent to a sacred oath that his life was inviolably secure. Was it only to gain the poor celebrity and fame, among the roving tribes around, of being murderess of a once illustrious soldier, that could be Deborah's meaning when she afterwards spoke of Jael as "Blessed," or famous, "above women in the tent?" (v. 24.) Among the wild sons of Ishmael her bloody deed may have been boastfully remembered and praised; but her name has no place among God's heroes, whose actions were afterwards lauded and enshrined in the psalms of the future singers of Israel. St. Paul speaks approvingly of a band of renowned warriors at this very age of Israel's history, but Jael is certainly not included in the roll-call, "who waxed valiant in fight, and turned to flight the armies of the aliens." I cannot say that the explanation is satisfactory that it was Jael's full and deliberate intention at first, when the wounded man put himself under her protection, to maintain faithfully her pledge of Arab fidelity; but that afterwards, she was seized by a sudden, incontrollable, or even divine impulse, to break her oath and murder the public enemy of Israel. "Honour 's a sacred tie, the law of kings." Another explanation, in the words of a judicious writer, is, that Deborah's language of commendation may have been used regarding her, "merely as one who acted a part in accomplishing an important purpose of heaven;—that in reality it is the work of God's judgment through her instrumentality that is celebrated, not her mode of carrying it into execution; and that it might be as just to regard the heathen Medes and Persians as a truly pious people, because they are called God's 'sanctified ones' to do His work of vengeance on Babylon, (Isaiah xiii. 3,) as from what is said in Deborah's song, to consider Jael an example of righteousness." We must leave the story as we find it, without venturing too confidently to vindicate, or too strongly to condemn.

We pass briefly to another of the shifting scenes in the drama. Barak, as Sisera had supposed, was in hot pursuit. For three days he and his warriors had been tracking the steps of the miserable fugitive: like bloodhounds, they have scented him at last to the tent of Jael the Kenite.

We can now picture the rival champion of Israel—drawing reins to his horse under "the oak of the wanderers." The wife of Heber advances outside the tent to meet him. She easily recognises her neighbour, and invites him to behold a spectacle which must have sorely marred the splendours of his triumph. In the savage spirit of the age (in which Israel was no exception) Barak would have desired either to secure the defeated warrior alive, to grace his triumph, or to have enjoyed the miserable satisfaction of being his assassin. Upon entering the tent, or upon Jael from outside drawing the curtain, he sees the body stretched on the ground, with the tent-peg still fast in his temples.

One other incident in the tragic event completes the story;—it is the return of the conquerors to their varied tribes and cities, bearing the spoil of the vanquished. Deborah's Hymn of praise was composed to be used on the occasion of this triumphal march; although it was not destined to be, like many such productions, an ephemeral composition—written for the hour and then forgotten. This prophetess of the Palm-tree was to take her place ever afterwards amid the ranks of the world's great poets,—the notes of her strain were to be sounded over all ages as one of the grandest of battle songs. The treasure upon which the Canaanites were so surely calculating is never to be theirs;

while, on the other hand, the wives and daughters of Israel are to be loaded with the spoil of Sisera's vast army. We can imagine with what joy the returning warriors would be welcomed in their several homes. It was a new era in the annals of the nation. It is likened, at the close of the song, to "the bursting out of the sun in his strength at early morning," (v. 31.) The Israelites may suffer, as we shall find they did, in future years from distant and foreign invasion;—but the last of the old heroic settlers, who had so long kept them in servitude, have been rooted from the soil—their chariots are left embedded in the mud of the Kishon. The name "Canaanite" is from this time forth unknown; and the land promised to their fathers, is now, from the length of it to the breadth of it, given to their children's children.

For forty years subsequently, the kingdom had rest; the deserted roads were repaired,—the deserted villages re-peopled: the sword and spear were changed into ploughshare and pruning-hook. The Judges of Israel could once more—now that they are delivered from all danger—"ride on their white asses," the token of honour and official dignity. They could now take their "seats of judgment" outside "the gates," seated on "the rich divans," or carpets of state;—and, better still, the villager who for years had to elude insult and violence by leaving the ways of traffic, and skulking by some secret by-path, could now walk fearlessly along the open thoroughfares. All these—even after the patriot writer was in her grave—would severally remember her words:—

> "Praise ye the Lord with me,
> Ye that ride upon the snow white asses;
> Ye that sit to judge on rich divans;
> Ye that plod on foot the open way,
> Come, meditate the song." *

The Canaanites were types of the enemies of God's Church in every age; while Deborah and Barak were similar types of those great Deliverers and Reformers who have from time to time risen to rescue her from spiritual bondage and degradation. However numerous, therefore, and powerful her foes may seem, God will raise up His own instruments at His own time and in His own way, for the protection of His people and the triumph of truth and righteousness. We can all join in the closing note of the song, "So let all thine enemies perish, O Lord!"

There is a reference made to this famous battle of Megiddo, which we have been describing, in one

* Dean Milman's translation.

of those inspired psalms of an after age, in which Jehovah is invoked, as the God of nations, to interpose in behalf of His oppressed people. His and their enemies are first spoken of; and then the description is followed by a sublime prayer. With this quotation I shall close our second "Tale of the Warrior-Judges:"—

"Thine enemies have said, Come, and let us cut them off from being a nation; that the name of Israel may be no more in remembrance. For they have consulted together with one consent; they are confederate against Thee. . . . Do unto them as to Sisera, as to Jabin, at the brook of Kison; which perished at En-dor; they became as dung for the earth. . . . O my God, make them like a wheel; as the stubble before the wind; yea, let them be put to shame and perish; that men may know that Thou, whose name alone is JEHOVAH, art the most High over all the earth," (Psalm lxxxiii. 4, 9, 17, 18.)

I have given the noble song of Deborah, in a disjointed form, in the pages preceding. Even at the risk of repetition, however, it may be well to present it as an unbroken whole. In doing so I shall avail myself of the most approved renderings and alterations of Hebrew scholars, who have made it their object to retain, at the same time, as much as possible, the structure and rhythm of the original. Many of my readers are doubtless familiar with some of the great war-songs found in the Greek and Latin languages, and especially in the writings of Homer and Virgil. Spirited as these are, none of them can be pronounced superior to this "*Epinikion*" of the old Hebrew poetess. The best authorities are at one in assigning to it, for force, grandeur, animation, and vivid description, the very highest place in lyric verse.

INTRODUCTION.—*The writer gives the key-note of the song—a preparatory strain, indicating her purpose and theme.*

Israel's mighty vengeance has been wrought;
The willing people rushed to battle:
Praise ye Jehovah!
Hear, ye kings; give ear, ye princes!
I to Jehovah, even I, will raise the song;
I will strike the harp to Jehovah, God of Israel.

THE GREAT VICTORY OF A FORMER AGE.—*She naturally begins by recalling the proudest memory of the Hebrew annals. It was the same God who led His people of old through the wilderness of Sinai who had again made bare His holy arm in the sight of the heathen.*

O Jehovah! when thou wentest forth from Seir,
When thou marchedst through the field of Edom,
Quaked the earth, and dropped down the heavens,
Yea, the clouds poured down water.
Before Jehovah's face the mountains melted,
Even Sinai itself, before Jehovah, Israel's God.

THE DESOLATION OF THE LAND.—*In order to enhance the greatness of the triumph, and the better to recognise Jehovah's hand in it, she describes how utterly demoralized and panic-stricken were the people immediately before the battle.*

In the days of Shamgar, son of Anath,
In the days of Jael,
Untrodden were the highways;
Through the winding by-path stole the traveller.
Deserted were the hamlets in Israel—ceased were they;
Until I Deborah arose,
Till I arose a mother in Israel.
They chose new gods,
Then there was war in all their gates:
Shield there was none, nor spear, seen among the forty thousand of Israel.

HER TRIBUTE OF THANKS TO THE VICTORIOUS ARMY.—*If such were the widespread desolation and dismay, all the greater gratitude is due to the brave men of all ranks who willingly offered themselves in the hour of peril.*

My soul beats towards you, ye chiefs of Israel,
And ye, the self-devoted of the people.
Praise Jehovah!

More especially does she call on the heads of the nation, who, by means of the signal victory, have had their state and their luxuries restored.

Ye who ride on white dappled she asses,
Ye who sit in judgment on rich divans,
Ye who travel along the highway,
Come, meditate the song.

THE CONTRAST.—*The writer proceeds to describe the peace and quiet which had followed a reign of terror. The women of Israel are now able to resume, without dread of the plundering foe, the drawing of water at the village fountains.*

Instead of the shouts of plundering archers at the wells of water,
We listen to the call,
"Come, rehearse Jehovah's righteous acts,
His righteous acts among the hamlets of Israel."

The gates of the cities were shut in the days of panic and plunder;—now they are open again, and the people may resort to them, as aforetime, for judgment.

Now they approach again the deserted gates, the people of Jehovah.

THE INVOCATION.—*By a sudden and beautiful transition she calls upon herself, as the minstrel of the occasion, to rise to the dignity of her theme; introducing also, appropriately, the name of the honoured leader of the armies of Israel.*

Awake, Deborah, awake!
Awake, awake, lift up the song!
Arise, Barak!
Lead thy captives captive,
Son of Abinoam.

THE MUSTER OF THE TRIBES.—*She praises the willing.*

A valiant few came down against the mighty,
Jehovah's people went down against the heroes;
First Ephraim, whose root is in Amalek;
After thee, Benjamin with his clan.
Out of Machir came lawgivers,
And out of Zebulun they that bear the staff;
Issachar's brave princes are with Deborah,
Issachar and Barak rush down into the valley.

The half-hearted and cowardly are rebuked.

By Reuben's streams there were great debatings;
Why sat'st thou idle among the sheepfolds?
Was it to hear the lowings of thy flocks?
At the streams of Reuben great are the searchings of heart.
Gilead, beyond the Jordan, lingers,
And Dan—why tarries he among his ships?
Asher sits by the sea-shore,
And reposes in his harbours.
But Zebulun and Naphtali throw away their lives
On the high places of the field.

THE BATTLE AND BATTLE-FIELD.—*The gathering of the Canaanites is described—and the rush of the tempest, which, in the hand of God, decided the fortunes of the day.*

There came the kings and fought;
The kings of Canaan fought
At Taanach, near Megiddo's waters,
For the golden booty they failed to win.

From the heavens they fought against Sisera,
The stars in their courses fought against him;
The stream Kishon swept them away,
The ancient torrent—the torrent Kishon.
So trample down, my soul, upon the mighty.

Then stamped the clattering hoofs of the war-horses
At the plungings, at the plungings of the valiant.

THE ROUT AND SLAUGHTER.—*This description begins with a curse on Meroz for standing aloof from the work of righteous vengeance.*

Curse ye Meroz, said the angel of Jehovah,
Curse, doubly curse, the inhabitants thereof,
For they came not to the succour of Jehovah,
To the succour of Jehovah against the mighty.

THE CAPTURE AND DEATH OF SISERA.—*The flight of the Canaanitish leader, and his tragical fate, are next described. Jael's conduct is contrasted with that of Meroz.*

Praised above all women be Jael,
The wife of the Kenite Heber;
Above all women in the tent blessed.
Water he asked. Milk she gave:
In a lordly bowl the curded milk.

Her hand she stretched out for the tent-peg,
Her right hand to the workman's mallet.
Then Sisera she smote,
She clave his head, she bruised and beat through his temples.

At her feet he bowed, he fell, he lay;
At her feet he bowed, he fell:
Where he bowed, there he lay dead.

THE EXPECTED BOOTY.—*The song effectively closes with the picture of Sisera's mother and her maidens watching the return of the conqueror, and counting the rich trophies he will lay at their feet.*

From the window she looked forth and cried—
The mother of Sisera—through the lattice:
"Why is his chariot so long in coming?
Wherefore tarry the wheels of his chariots?"

Her wise women answer her—
Yea, she herself replies to her own question:
"Surely they are taking, they are dividing the spoil—
One damsel—two damsels for each chief;
Spoil of divers colours for Sisera,
A many-coloured robe of embroidery,
One of divers hues—embroidered for the neck."

THE CLOSING VERSE OF THE SONG.—*Imprecation against Jehovah's foes, and a blessing on His children.*

So perish all thine enemies, O Jehovah!
But may those that love thee be as the sun
When he goeth forth in his glory!

Gideon and his Servant Phurah Stealing down by Night to the Camp of the Midianites.

III.

STORY OF GIDEON.

BARAK and Deborah, Josephus informs us, died about the same time. But at the end of the forty years' peace, which they were the happy means of securing, a new enemy ravaged the territories of Israel.

Heroic as Deborah undoubtedly was, she must resign the first place among "the Warrior-Judges" to the great champion now raised up to be the leader of Israel in the most sanguinary war recorded in Hebrew history. There is, what may almost be called, a romantic and pictorial interest attached to this campaign; we need hardly wonder that it lived so long in the national annals, and was engraved with such pride in the national memory—recalled by prophets, and sung by psalmists. The invasion itself, before it was bravely repelled, must have infused a terror resembling that inspired by the irruption of the Goths, Visigoths, and Vandals, when they inundated with their hordes the civilized nations of Europe. It would doubtless form the favourite war-tale of Hebrew youth—dividing, at all events, their attention with the chivalrous story of the Red Sea and the Wilderness. In varied and thrilling adventure it is not exceeded by the heroic exploits of David in after years. Its only parallel, perhaps, in dramatic grandeur, was the yet far off descent of the Assyrian Sennacherib, "the eagle," who afterwards made his nest on the cedars of Lebanon.

The present multitude of invaders, who are now to occupy our attention, came from the mysterious land (mysterious even to this day) on the other side of the Jordan. They consisted of "the Midianites and Amalekites, and the *Bene-kedem*," or "Children of the East." To use a term of the Middle Ages, it may be regarded as a vast *crusade* of the wild Arabs of the wild desert against the peaceful and unoffending Israelites. The Midianites formed the main body. It may be difficult to assign, geographically, the territory which this Bedouin race claimed specially as their own. We cannot be wrong in describing it as bordering on the eastern frontier of Palestine, and stretching to the southern end of the Dead Sea. Doubtless, however, it extended much farther than this, as we know from the Bible narrative that they roamed the green pasture lands in the peninsula of Sinai. They have justly been described as the most "nomadic"—in other words, the most roving and unsettled—of all the sons of the desert. They had probably secured the co-operation of these other powerful tribes just mentioned, in case the latter, during their absence, might be tempted to commit depredations on their own territories. They would be able also thus to ensure, by an overwhelming force, the final conquest of Israel. The oldest foe of the wandering Hebrews—the tribe of Amalek—we may be sure, would not be unwilling to settle former grudges and resent former humiliations. The word Midian is said to mean "strife" or "contention;"—and they were, not only now, but had always been, true to their name and character. They had proved in previous times one of the most dangerous of the enemies of Israel, alike in the arts of war, and in the equally fatal arts of corruption and wickedness. The very last injunction Moses himself received from the lips of God, ere he ascended

Mount Pisgah to his grave, was this, "Avenge the children of Israel of the Midianites," (Numbers xxxi. 2.) Faithfully and terribly was the Divine command fulfilled. We are expressly informed that twelve thousand picked soldiers of the Hebrews razed to the ground their "cities and goodly castles," (Numbers xxxi. 10.) It further gives an impression of what a powerful tribe Midian must have been, when we read of the amount of booty taken from them, alike in herds and in money. In flocks, no less than 575,000 sheep, 72,000 oxen, and 61,000 asses. In "specie" and valuables, besides "silver, brass, iron, tin, and lead," there were 16,750 shekels of gold and costly jewels, (Num. xxxi. 22, 52.) A period of two hundred years, however, had now elapsed since that punishment and repulse was inflicted on them. Their children had restored and rebuilt the dismantled castles and fortresses. They had anew amassed enormous riches; perhaps succeeded in recovering some of the very spoil of which they had been deprived by the Hebrews. The wave that had been beaten back had gathered fresh strength to renew the assault. For a period of seven years the Israelites had been subjected to constant invasions from these foraging Bedouins. The latter knowingly allowed the former to plough and sow their fields in winter and spring; but the ripening corn in early summer, or as the harvest season approached, was the signal for their advance, and they located themselves in the most favoured spots of Palestine until the autumn fruits were gathered. The rich fields of Esdraelon formed the special object of their plunder. They obtained comparatively easy access to these by the fords of Bethshan on the Jordan. They approached them on their fleet horses by the lesser plain of Jezreel, and were instigated to merciless rapacity by the martial summons or war-cry of their chiefs, as given us in one of the Psalms, "Seize these goodly pastures," (Psalm lxxxiii. 12,) (Stanley's *Lectures;* also Dr. Smith, *Art.* "*Zebah.*") Or, as that has perhaps rather been rendered, as implying a scoffing and ironical allusion to the Divine Protector of the Hebrews,—"Seize these pastures *of God.*" * They advanced, we are told in the narrative in Judges, in such numbers, that they could only be likened to the devastating plague of locusts. They darkened the earth with their black tents, as these darken the air in their flight;—their flocks were let loose in the standing corn; their camels—something

* The translation in our Authorized Version is, "Let us take to ourselves the houses of God in possession."

novel to the eye of the Hebrew since the days of Egypt and the desert—are specially spoken of as being numerous "as the sand by the sea," (Judges vii. 12.) These latter animals were of evil omen to the Israelites; for, as "ships of the desert," they were freighted by the robber gangs with the produce of this granary of Palestine. Their owners decamped to their own territory, "with all manner of store," to enjoy the ill-gotten gains, or wantonly destroyed what they could not carry away. The Israelites, you will at once see, had good reason to renew the groan of Egypt under these fresh task-masters. They found, to their consternation, their crops wasted "even to Gaza," on the Mediterranean. The enemy "destroyed the increase of the land, and left no sustenance, neither sheep, nor ox, nor ass," (Judges vi. 4.) As a natural and inevitable result, a famine followed: the same famine, it is supposed, which is spoken of in the Book of Ruth, and which compelled Elimelech and Naomi to take refuge with their children in the land of Moab—leaving Bethlehem, which, like the rest of the country, had become untrue to its name, "The House of Bread." At no period of the Jewish history were the sufferings of the population apparently greater. Like the early

Roman Christians in their catacombs, or like the Vaudois of the middle centuries in their rocky caverns, they had to retreat for safety from the invaders to places of refuge. Palestine then, as now, was full of natural caves. Some of these, in its limestone formations, were so large, as to be capable of containing a little army; and, if supplied with provisions and other necessaries, could bid stubborn defiance for a long period to a numerous host. In the southern portion of the Holy Land, perhaps the most familiar are those of Adullam and Engedi, those at Mar-Saba in the gorge of the Kedron, and those at the Wady Kelt and Quarantania, overlooking the plains of Jericho. A writer mentions, that even at the present day the shepherds around Hebron are in the habit of leaving their homes in summer, and taking up their abode in caves, in order to be nearer their flocks, (*Robinson.*) In the north it is the same. Gadara, on the eastern shore of the Sea of Tiberias, is filled with sepulchral caves or cavities, in one of which the maniac of old dwelt: these still form, indeed, the habitations of the wild population, (*Burckhardt*, p. 273.) The same traveller mentions some caves—famous haunts of robbers—on the opposite shore, near Magdala, called the Pigeon's Castle, capable of containing six hundred men. Josephus relates of one of these, that it was held by bandits in the reign of Herod. That king ordered his soldiers to attack the gang —a formidable exploit, which could only be accomplished by lowering the assaulting party from the cliffs above, in cages or baskets. They succeeded in the feat—dragging forth the robbers with iron hooks—hurling some down the precipices, and, by setting fire to their stores of fuel, suffocating others, (*Smith*, *Art.* "*Caves.*") Though not so adapted for purposes of defence, the most remarkable of all these caverns is the enormous subterranean cavity which, comparatively recently, has been discovered under Jerusalem itself. It is entered near the Damascus gate, and would be capable of containing several thousand men. To it, and to some adjoining caves, hundreds of Jews fled from the miseries of famine and the sword, at the siege of Jerusalem by the army of Titus. Of these shelters and mountain clefts the oppressed Israelites, at the time of which I write, availed themselves. Not a few, according to Josephus, even crept into holes in the ground, and there dragged out a miserable life; others went to "strongholds,"—"munitions of rocks," forts built on high and inaccessible cliffs,—where, for a time at least, they could bid defiance to the fury of the invaders. Dr. Thomson, in his interesting *Land and the Book*, speaking of the resemblance between ancient depredators in the plain of Esdraelon, and those of the present day, remarks, "In precisely the same manner do the Bedouin Arabs, these modern Midianites, come up the Wady of Jezreel and Wady Sherrer, after the people have sown, and destroy the increase of the earth." Another picture of a comparatively modern writer, just quoted,—describing Bedouin incursions and devastations in this century, still more vividly reproduces the state of things in that age of Hebrew history. "In May, the whole Hauran is covered with swarms of wanderers from the deserts, who remain there till September. They come for a twofold purpose—water and pasturage for the summer, and a supply of corn for the winter. The oppressions of the Government on the one hand, and of these Bedouins on the other, have reduced the fellah (cultivator) to a state little better than that of the wandering Arabs. Few individuals die in the same village where they were born. Families are continually moving from one place to another. In the first year of their new settlement, the sheikh acts with moderation towards them;

but his vexations being in a few years insupportable, they fly to some other place, where they have heard that their brethren are better treated; but they soon find that the same system prevails over the whole country. This continued wandering is one of the principal reasons why no village of the Ḥauran has either orchards, or fruit trees, or gardens for the growth of vegetables. 'Shall we sow for strangers?' was the answer of a fellah to whom I once spoke on the subject," (Burckhardt's *Travels in Syria*, quoted by Dr. Kitto, p. 306-8.)

The greatest and most gigantic of all these forays took place at the close of these seven years.

Up that same pass I have already spoken of, swarmed the Midianites and their Bedouin allies. The vast host of marauders is encamped on the southern slopes of the hills which bound the north-east portion of the plain of Esdraelon. Conspicuous in the compact horde are the tall figures of their chiefs. Four of these are mentioned by name. Zebah and Zalmunna would seem to occupy the position, equivalent at least, to King. They were the higher chiefs or emirs—the same who are called by the title of Sheikh-el-kebîr at the present day.* The two latter are named Oreb and Zeeb—princes

* Dr. Smith's *Bible Dictionary, Art.* "*Zalmunna.*"

too, but evidently subordinate to the others in rank. Oreb literally means "raven" or "crow"—Zeeb, "wolf." The Bedouins were in the habit of conferring distinctive appellations on their warrior leaders, appropriate to their natural character, and indicative of their gifts or their special exploits. Indeed the custom has been common in all martial times. To take two examples which occur at random—that of the English Richard "of the lion-heart," of crusader fame; or that of the lawless Scottish chieftain, also a king's son, whose ferocious habits and cruelties carried terror among the northern clans,—remarkable as being the identical name conferred on this Midianite chief—"the wolf of Badenoch."* In the details afterwards given of the spoils of victory, we are able to add other touches to the brilliant picture drawn in the Book of Judges, (viii. 25-27.) These chiefs and their retainers had come arrayed in all that costly magnificence peculiar to the East. We imagine the former, seated aloft on the back of their camels and dromedaries, attired in robes of gorgeous purple, bespangled with orna-

* Dr. Stanley notes, as a curious circumstance, that "the title of 'The Leopard' is given to Abd el Aziz, the modern successor of Oreb and Zeeb—chief of the Bedouins beyond Jordan;" (*Sinai and Palestine*, p. 337.)

ments,—massive golden collars on their necks, and circular ear-rings. Nor is this splendour confined to the riders. The very dromedaries are covered with carpets of golden tissue, and chains are suspended from their long necks. If the ear-rings subsequently gathered, alone amounted in weight to 1700 shekels, (viii. 26,) we may bring before our imagination the imposing aggregate of all that "barbaric pearl and gold" which gleamed in the mid-day sun before the eyes of the Israelites, who were encamped on the opposite side of the plain.

From the vast disparity in numbers, it would seem little short of madness for the handful of the Hebrew people to attempt attacking so gigantic a foe. If the bold venture, however, dare be made, everything would depend, as in the former great battle, on procuring a brave and skilful leader. Leaving for a little the spectacle of the hordes of Midian, with their blaze of gorgeous colours, we shall make our young readers familiar with the illustrious champion whom the God of Israel raised up for the momentous struggle.

Ophrah, a small town or village somewhere among the hills of Manasseh—surrounded with vineyards, (vi. 11,) possibly not far from the battle-field of Megiddo—was the birthplace of GIDEON. Who knows, but the scene of that former fight, if thus from boyhood familiar to him, may have nurtured within his soul great thoughts; and, when the hour of his own call to duty arrived, may have nerved his arm for even grander exploits. If the surmise as to the situation of Ophrah be correct,* he could not, at all events, during these seven long years of which I have spoken, watch from the heights of his village home, without burning indignation, the ravaging of the fertile plain below. Harvest after harvest the fruitful field became a wilderness. But, amid these high thoughts of patriotism evoked by the wrongs of his country and people, we must not omit to note other considerations and impulses of a personal kind; for if we overlook these, we lose the key and explanation to much of the future of our story. A more terrible crime (demanding a more terrible vengeance, even than the devastation of fields and villages) was locked up, like a heavy secret, in the soul of Gideon.

Let me explain it. If not conspicuous from the place of his birth, at all events conspicuous

* The site of Gideon's native place must, however, from the meagre allusions to it in the sacred narrative, be conjectural. Some are disposed to place it farther in the interior, nearer Shechem.

from the slopes of his native hills, was the conical top of Mount Tabor, where, you remember, the hosts of Barak and Deborah were encamped. On that green platform, the Midian chiefs, now heading the Arab army, had caught his three prince-like brothers, and murdered them in cold blood, leaving him the alone survivor of a once happy household. We need not pause at present to speak of how diametrically opposed the old law of blood revenge is to the spirit and precepts of the Gospel. But it was a code which Israelite and Bedouin held in common. Nay, the former, under the Mosaic dispensation, had even Divine sanction for carrying its penalties into execution. That stern law was unrepealed—"An eye for an eye, and a tooth for a tooth,"—"Whosoever sheddeth man's blood, by man shall his blood be shed." Moreover, there was a special injunction regarding the inflictor of vengeance, which belonged to the code alike of Israelite and Ishmaelite. The nearest of kin to the murdered had the awful necessity laid upon him to avenge the blood, whose "voice" (to use the oldest phrase of the Bible) "cried from the ground." Gideon *might* overlook these depredations committed on the territories of Israel, or leave to others the task of retribution,—but he could never let sleep the retaliation demanded for the massacre of his brethren. The vision of Tabor, with its deed of horror, would haunt him night and day. In giving this matter of personal insult and wrong such prominence in the narrative, we do not in any degree detract from the nobler features in his heroism. We willingly do homage to his love of country, his high-minded patriotism; these indeed may have been the motives and feelings which predominated during the heat of the stupendous battle itself;—but if we would understand fully the sequel—the desperation with which he followed the retreating foe, we shall find the true explanation, in his resolve to avenge the personal wrong and outrage—to wipe out the indignity offered to himself and his father's house with the blood of the Midian murderers.

As we found the name Deborah probably derived from a word which signifies "a bee," so the name Gideon means literally "hewer;" and he is considered by some to have been called so, in anticipation of his terrible duty—as the hewer, the avenger, the slayer.

We can form a pleasing picture of his appearance. He was the youngest of the family. Each of his brothers, as well as himself, we are told, "resembled the children of a king," (Judges viii. 18.) In other words, he was handsome—of royal mien, like Saul among the people. As was the case with that first monarch of Israel, or with Absalom, who—the one by his colossal proportions, the other by his gracefulness of person—stole the hearts of the people, Gideon may have owed his advancement and after popularity in no small measure to these external qualities, which have always bulked so largely in the eyes of Orientals. Although the battle of Midian is the only one in which we read of his being personally engaged, it is by no means improbable, from the words with which the angel afterwards saluted him, that he was no stranger to brave deeds and bold adventure—"Thou mighty man of valour." He had an ample school and opportunity of training for future generalship, in the sudden sallies he would doubtless already have been tempted to make, in repelling the insolence of the Bedouin. In another sense, however, he would seem to have been, like his ancestor Jacob, "a plain man." He tells us himself he was of a "poor" family. Probably his occupation was that of a husbandman—cultivating the paternal acres, tending the crops, and watching the progress of the vines on the hill-slope.

Gideon had one son, by name Jether, whom we

shall afterwards meet with, ere the narrative is closed.

With the remembrance of Tabor, then, before his mental eye, and its deep wound rankling in his heart; his country, moreover, bleeding at every pore—GIDEON—the mighty man—the valorous prince—"every inch a king," is only waiting a higher summons to be ready for the great enterprise. The hour and the call have come.

The scene which now presents itself is a domestic one; but it surely gives a touching insight into the distress and misery, the terror, oppression, and dismay, that had fallen on Israel, when we find even Gideon—this elect hero (living, too, not in the plain, but in an upland village) threshing out, by stealth, his father's newly reaped corn. For this purpose he does not use the ordinary threshing-floor, —that being generally in an exposed place. A flat plot of hard earth or clay close to the field where the grain was cut down, and watched by evil eyes, might make both him and it a prey to the Midian plunderers; but he has conveyed the wheat that has just fallen to the sickle to the wine-press, away in a retired place among the vineyards, where no one could ever suspect it to be,—the vintage presses being in use only at the vintage season. Moreover, the winnowed grain fell into a hollow underneath, through a hole in the press—the same aperture through which the juice of the grape, at the time of grape-gathering, flowed into vats or casks placed to receive it in the cavity below. It further denotes the extreme secrecy which was needful in carrying on the operation. The usual method of treading out the corn, either by the feet of oxen or by means of detached logs of wood drawn along and bruising it, would have created too much noise, and apprized the vigilant watchers of the hidden spoil. Accordingly, it is implied in the original that Gideon used the ordinary flail, this being less likely than the lowing kine to raise suspicion, and carry the secret to the predatory tyrants. It must be further remembered, too, as a discriminating writer notes, (Dr. Kitto,) that the threshing of the Israelites, where the flail was the instrument employed, was accompanied with little or no noise, such as we are accustomed to hear in the wooden floors of our barns at home. It would be a dull deadened sound, that would scarcely reach the outskirts of the vineyard. Still less, perhaps, would the Midianites dream of corn being deposited in such a place, seeing, as is further evident from the narrative, that it was a religious spot, having a grove of sacred trees, or as some think, with an image crowning the summit of the rock. It gives us, indeed, a deplorable picture of the declension of Israel, at this time, from the faith of their fathers, that even the family of the appointed champion of His people were worshippers of Baal and Astarte. Retired as the spot was, and apparently situated in the private vineyard of Joash, the father of Gideon, it seems thus to have been the sanctuary or holy place of the village, whither the inhabitants were wont to resort for their devotional rites. This has led to the surmise that Joash himself may have been the officiating priest of the false worship.

While thus engaged, an Angel of God—a glorious being, evidently of supreme dignity—suddenly appears, with the salutation, "The Lord is with thee, thou mighty man of valour!" Gideon is at first startled at the unwonted apparition; but being reassured, he bemoans to the messenger the disastrous condition to which the nation had been reduced. He cannot resist giving vent to Atheist doubts as to Israel's God being true to His chosen people: "Oh my lord, if the Lord be with us, why then is all this befallen us?" The angel comforts him. According to Josephus, "he told him he was happy and beloved of God." At all events, he informed him of his commission to be the accredited leader of Israel against the Midianites, who, moreover, are to be utterly overthrown:—"Go in this thy might, and thou shalt save Israel from the hand of the Midianites: have not I sent thee?" The dignity of his visitor is revealed to Gideon through a miraculous sign—viz., by fire rising from the rock close by. The mysterious messenger vanishes from sight; and the son of Joash—awe-struck and solemnized—yet confident and assured—sets up, then and there, an altar with the inscription, *Jehovàh-shalom*—"the peace of Jehovah," or "Jehovah gives peace."

I shall not prolong this story by describing fully the first act of the drama. This did not consist in Gideon's marching direct to the battle-field, and, with the blast of trumpets, summoning all Israel to the strife; but rather in fulfilling a prior Divine injunction. By a bold and significant act, he wipes away the dishonour done to the true God by the existence of Baal worship. In a dream the same night, he is directed to overthrow the altar of Baal, and to hew down with the axe either image or grove, or possibly both. It was a bold exploit; for he well knew how dangerous, as it always is, to tamper with religious feelings and prejudices. In the present case, the penalty was stoning to death.

But, armed with such authority, and recognising the call and injunction to be of God, he does not hesitate. Selecting the dead of night, and in concert with ten faithful servants, he proceeded to effect the demolition. He levels alike altar, and grove, and idol; and with the wood of the former he presents a burnt-offering of a bullock to Jehovah. In that silent hour and place, the future cry is anticipated that was heard on a hill, not far off, when Baal's altars were once more overthrown—"The Lord, He is the God; the Lord, He is the God!" When the morning dawns there is nothing left but the white ashes of the sacrifice. The villagers, on the discovery, are furious with rage. They demand of the father immediate punishment for the sacrilege committed by his son—"Bring forth thy son, that he may die." Joash, however, adopted a sensible plan of appeasing the indignation of his fellow-townsmen. It was briefly this,—'If Baal has been insulted, he will take care of his own wounded dignity. He is quite able for his own defence, and to vindicate his own majesty. If he cannot resent the affront by some immediate vengeance falling on my son, it shews him to be no god; and if such be the case, you surely will not continue to plead for him:' "Will ye plead for Baal? Let Baal plead for himself." The device was happily successful in appeasing the enraged votaries. The angry crowd dispersed. It was, moreover, the occasion of a new title being conferred on the future hero of his country. The name Gideon was exchanged for that of *Jerubbaal*, which means, "Let Baal plead." This surname of the Phenician Hercules, now adopted by a son of Abraham, would go down to posterity, reminding of the fact of Baal's impotence, and the triumph of Jehovah's messenger and servant.

Gideon seems now all prepared for his great undertaking. Yet, seeing his call was so sudden, and the achievement to be accomplished so vast and superhuman, we cannot wonder that his wavering faith should, before setting out, demand from the God he obeyed some visible sign. The old words with which at first he addressed the angel, seem still to cling to him. "Oh my Lord, wherewith shall *I* save Israel? behold, my family is poor in Manasseh, and I am the least in my father's house." And, truly, if the village of Ophrah was situated, as we have imagined, on some spur or height of the Manasseh hills, overlooking the plain of Esdraelon, we need not be surprised that the bravest heart would have its misgivings, when moving masses of armed men were seen stretched along the wide valley for miles, as far as the eye could reach. It was a singular, but yet a natural and appropriate sign which the young husbandman of Ophrah ventured to ask of the Great Being who had called him. Dews, as is well known, are far more copious in Palestine than in our country. Gideon took the fleece of one of his sheep, and, spreading it out in the evening on the ground, he asked, as the token of his being Divinely commissioned, that in the morning the ground all round might be found dry, while the fleece alone was saturated with moisture; and when this sign was graciously granted, he was bold enough to prefer that the next night it should be reversed—that on the second morning the ground would be found drenched with dew and the fleece miraculously dry. Both pledges of the Divine presence and aid being accorded to him, he sallied forth, without one misgiving, to the path of duty and victory; this, I need not say, being the secret of his strength, and of his ultimate triumph—"The Spirit of the Lord came upon Gideon," (literally "clothed him," as with a suit of armour,) (Judges vi. 34.)

And now commences the assembling of his own troops. In the first instance it is confined to the northern tribes. He blows his rough war-trumpet, and the mustering commences with a response from his own clan—"Abi-ezer was gathered after him." The trumpet is again sounded by special messengers sent here and there throughout the tribe of Manasseh. The circle is enlarged by including the warlike men of Zebulun and Naphtali, who answered, it will be remembered, so cordially in the former struggle to the summons of Deborah. Asher, who then selfishly clung to his ships, and preferred ease to duty, is at present among the enrolled number. These four northern tribes contribute 32,000 fighting men. Judah, as on the last occasion also, is absent. Even the great tribe of Ephraim had no place in the ranks. This, however, did not arise from any unwillingness, apathy, or cowardice on their part, but rather from having received no invitation—a neglect which we shall find them afterwards angrily resenting. "It is worthy of remark," says Dr. Thomson, "that the men of Issachar are not mentioned, and we can readily imagine the reason. The people of Issachar lived on this great plain, and were, of course, altogether surrounded by, and at the mercy of the Midianites, as the villages of Sulam, Shutta, Zarin, &c., now are in the power of the Bedouin. They therefore could not join the army of Gideon,"

(*Land and the Book.*) The muster seems to have taken place at Ophrah. Early one summer morning they are in motion, and take up their ground face to face with the enemy. The place of Israel's encampment, we are told in the narrative of Judges, was beside the well of Harod or Jezreel—the modern Ain Jahlood—"the spring of Goliath." We may accurately describe their position as at the far east end of Esdraelon, on the northern slope of the Hill of Gilboa—the same grey, bare. rounded mountain that was to have a sadder association, in an after age, as the scene of the death of Saul and Jonathan, where "the shield of the mighty was cast vilely away." "The host of Midian was beneath in the valley." They must have covered, as I have previously said, with their dense multitude, a large portion of the plain itself, besides the slopes of the adjoining hills; but the centre of the army—the royal tents, (probably constituting the flower of their soldiers,)—was "by the Hill of Moreh," on the slopes of what is known in modern times as "Little Hermon," a barer, and much less conspicuous mountain than the great Hermon, whose base formed the muster-ground of Barak's troops in the last campaign.

But what are these undisciplined 32,000, against

the "135,000 men that drew sword," now confronting them in all the pomp and circumstance of Eastern war? Yet, strange to say, even these 32,000 are to be subjected to successive diminutions, till Gideon is left with the merest handful. The God of the Hebrews is about to magnify His own great name in the coming struggle, and the command is given to the hero, "The people that are with thee are too many, . . . lest Israel vaunt themselves against me, saying, Mine own hand hath saved me." The trumpets are therefore again sounded, and what is supposed to have been an old war-cry of the Manasseh tribe, is proclaimed among the ranks, "Whosoever is fearful and afraid, let him return and depart early from Mount Gilead." A large proportion avail themselves of the exemption. Alas! it shews how much of the brave old heroic spirit of Israel had died out, that the cowards should so outnumber the brave. No less than 20,000 are seen rushing back to their homes, while 10,000 alone remain standing in their ranks.

But the winnowing fan is yet again to be applied,—another still more remarkable diminution is yet to take place. The valour even of that apparently faithful 10,000 is not to be depended upon.

According to Josephus, "God appeared to Gideon in his sleep, and advised him to bring his army at noon, in the violence of the heat, to the side of the river," which divided them from the Midianites. By a remarkable test he was there to ascertain who among his ranks would prove serviceable and intrepid, and who, by lagging behind, would only impede the dashing effort by which, God helping them, the battle was to be won. Gideon accordingly, under the Divine direction, led his troops down to the water side. Those of them who stood upright and lapped the water as they drank, were comparatively few. The bulk of the soldiers got down upon their knees and leisurely slaked their thirst. The action of the former indicated impetuosity, celerity of movement, a readiness to meet and to rough difficulties—just what was required for the sudden attack that was to decide the fortunes of the war. The slowness and deliberation of the others would have been fatal to the night exploit, in which everything depended on promptitude and intrepidity. Those, then, who stood upright—throwing the water into their mouths with a sound that resembled the lapping of a dog—although only 300 in number, were set aside as the "forlorn hope" in the attack, while those who adopted the kneeling posture were disbanded.

The shades of evening have gathered in, and Gideon and his 300 picked men await further directions from heaven. A Divine voice instructs him to go alone, in company with Phurah his armour-bearer, in the darkness, (when the mighty host of Midian are asleep,) to receive some further tokens of encouragement ere the onset take place. Gideon's previous sign was a personal request. The present is given him unsolicited. He obeys the Divine direction. The two warriors sally down at midnight, from what might well have been called "the spring of trembling," towards the city of tents in the plain beneath. The precise object of this nocturnal visit had not been disclosed to them. They must have wondered to themselves what its upshot would be; whether it was simply, what is called, to *reconnoitre*—that is, to ascertain the best point of assault. It could not fail, at all events, to be a thrilling sight which was disclosed to them, for we are told that "the Children of the East lay along the valley like grasshoppers for multitude." Some of that teeming throng may have but recently crossed the fords of Jordan. Some may have that day returned from one of their numerous raids among the peaceful plains and villages of Israel, loaded with booty and plunder. But all were now locked in slumber—with many it would be needed rest. Nothing would be heard but the occasional trampling and neighing of the horses—nothing seen but the weird forms of camels and dromedaries; some moored like ships around the tents, others towering in the glow of the watch-fires, or dimly revealed in the bright star-light. The reason of the stealthy mission is soon explained. In reaching the tent, probably of one of the out-posts, and creeping as near as safety would permit, Gideon was able, unobserved, to listen to a conversation which took place between two of the sentinels who were just relieving watch. The one, roused from his sleep, tells to his fellow the substance of a remarkable dream, from which the other had just awoke him. He dreamt that from the top or slope of one of these southern hills which fronted their armies, he saw a cake of barley-meal come rolling down, and never pausing in its course till it "tumbled into the host of Midian," striking against a tent (or in the original, "*the* tent"—the *royal* one) it overturned it, and caused it to lie flat on the ground. Josephus describes the appearance of the cake as "a vile one, hardly to be eaten;" and we know that barley-bread was and is regarded by the Orientals as the meanest fare, and often, on that account, given to prisoners.* The brother soldier seemed at no loss for an interpretation. He immediately replied that the barley-cake was "the sword of Gideon, the son of Joash—a man in Israel," for "into his hand God had delivered Midian and all his host."

Gideon does not require any further confirmation. He pauses only to do obeisance to the God who had conducted him thither, and afforded him so distinct and unmistakeable a pledge. "He worshipped;" and then, plunging into the darkness, he and his companion steal back in silence as they had descended, to rejoin their small but brave troop. If he had any misgivings before, these have now vanished. He has become acquainted with the significant and important fact from the soldier's dream, that his name was already a source of fear and panic to the Midianites. On mere human calculations, this circumstance alone would have tended to impart

* "Barley-bread is only eaten by the *poor* and the *unfortunate.* Nothing is more common than for these people, at this day, to complain that their oppressors have left them nothing but *barley-bread* to eat. I remember that this was the identical lamentation of a wealthy farmer who rode with me from Zirin to Jevîn. This cake of barley-bread was therefore naturally supposed to belong to the oppressed Israelites." (Dr. Thomson's "*Land and the Book.*")

hopeful confidence. But far more than this. The dream had given him the direct guarantee that the Lord of Hosts was with him, and that he might prepare his tactics or stratagems in the assurance of victory. His 300 were apparently waiting, all armed and ready for battle. They leap to their feet, as he welcomes them on his return with the words, "Arise; for the Lord hath delivered into your hand the host of Midian."

And how does Gideon conduct the great assault? With what possible manœuvring or stratagem can 300 men put 135,000 to flight? That was the problem he had to solve; and his solution was alike strange, ingenious, original, and successful,—unlike anything that has ever occurred in the world's greatest battles before or since. To have encountered them with the regular weapons of war in open day—however desperate might be their feats of bravery—was utterly hopeless. The object which, with rare tactics, Gideon had in view, was to avail himself of the terror easily produced by a sudden surprise in the dark, on huge masses of men, and especially among those largely influenced by superstitious dread, as was pre-eminently the case with these 'Children of the East.' Into the right hand of each of his 300 he puts a ram's horn or trumpet, and in their left an earthen pot or pitcher, in which was placed a lighted torch. These pitchers were such as were used by the Israelites for holding any of the common necessaries of life—water, bread, or meal. Gideon's troops being volunteers, these household jars would be the most ready and available for each soldier carrying any needful provisions for the sudden emergency—and would, in this sense, so far correspond with the modern 'kit,' 'canteen,' or 'knapsack.' The little band he divides into three companies, a hundred in each, and instructs them to approach the Midianitish camp from three different quarters. Josephus says it was about the fourth watch of the night when they sallied forth on their enterprise. On a concerted signal, the scattered troop of Israelites broke their pitchers with a sudden noise. The torches concealed in them, in an instant were flaming in the darkness, while the blast of the trumpets mingled with the crashing of the pitchers; and then, loud above crash and blast, rose the grand battle-cry, "The sword of the Lord and of Gideon!" Gideon had been taught, one-half at least of that memorable war-shout, as he listened to the interpreter of the Midianitish soldier's dream,—"The sword of Gideon the son of Joash." But he adds to the

Bedouin version of it another name than his own, or rather he gives that name the precedence. In the victory impending, he wishes to testify that he has "no glory by reason of the glory that excelleth;" and therefore the pious exclamation wakes the silent echoes of these Esdraelon hills, "The sword of *the Lord* and of Gideon." A noble battle-song truly, which has a poor rendering given it by Josephus, "Victory to Gideon by God's assistance." It was used in other and future great conflicts of the world: whether, as the historian Xenophon tells us, by one, like-minded to Gideon in magnanimity and bravery, Cyrus—the best of Persian kings;—or amid the wild rocks of the Cottian Alps by the hunted Albigenses. We can feebly imagine the result in the present case. That vast congregation of sleepers, roused in a moment by unearthly noises, the din of crashing pitchers and the shout of Israel, —the latter always "like the shout of a king,"— and then, no sooner do they start from their pillows, (be it from the bare sod covered by the black war-tents—or the embroidered divans within royal curtains,) than they see, for miles around, plain and mountain luminous with flaring torches, as if the demons of the hills or of the distant sea had been let loose upon them on an errand of vengeance. Nor would it be the *soldiers* of Midian alone that would share in the consternation. In these predatory incursions of the Arab tribes, there was always a large number of sutlers and camp followers, not to speak of women and children—indeed a promiscuous mass of human beings, all now involved in a wild and incontrollable panic; while the vast herds and flocks kept for the sustenance of the army, the fleet and nervous horses of the Arab cavalry, and the camels and dromedaries, (used both for saddle and for baggage,) becoming unmanageable amid the moving lights—would rush madly about, spreading and increasing the alarm. Josephus specially notes the number of their camels. These would prove like the iron chariots of the Canaanites at the Kishon, a trouble and encumbrance, and, as in the former case, what they thus most relied upon, would become a principal cause of confusion, disaster, and defeat. The result was not left long doubtful: 300 trumpets, sounding all at once in different directions, conveyed to the roused host the impression that there were a corresponding number of companies all closing in upon them. Every sort of wild exaggerated terror would take hold of them. The encircling ring of flame would carry the tale from lip to lip that the encampments were fired, that the conflagration would speedily spread through the dry rank herbage, till every tent was enveloped in the blaze. The breaking of the pitchers would sound to some like the clash of arms, to others like the sound of chariot wheels, or the jingle of horse-gear rushing to battle, while the ever-approaching cries and shouting betokened the nearness of the enemy. The bewilderment of being suddenly roused from sleep, coupled with the gloom of the night, produced confusion worse confounded. The slaughter had begun; not, however, from the weapons of Gideon's men. The panic-stricken multitudes, in their delirium and despair, turned their swords against one another, imagining, in the darkness of that darkest watch, that they were encountering the enemy, when in truth "every man's sword was against his fellow." The diversity in the tribes which composed this vast Arab mob, and which, under the wide term "Children of the East," implies endless variety in dress, costume, weapons, even language, would render it very difficult to discriminate between friend and foe. The rout was complete. No battle could be more graphically described than in these three expressions in the sacred narrative, "all the host ran, and cried, and fled," (Judges vii. 21.) Many thousands were left dead on the field, while the remnant, headed by their chiefs, retreated down to the fords of Jordan. With some, doubtless, the retreat would be precipitate; with the greater number, however, this was impossible. The gigantic host must have been encumbered with its beasts of burden; and the camel, of all animals, is least capable of accommodating its slow and stately movements to a headlong flight. They halted at two places somewhere down in that deep gorge under the hills of Ephraim, called Beth-shitta, "the house of the acacia," and Abel-meholah, "the meadow of the dance;"—the latter being the same place which had a more peaceful association in a future age, for it was the spot where Elijah the Tishbite found Elisha at his plough, and called him to be his successor in the prophetical office. By this time morning has dawned, and ere the day is passed, Gideon feels he must follow up his miraculous victory. His own handful is quite insufficient for the purpose, besides being wearied ("faint") with the long midnight manœuvre. He first of all sends tidings of the rout to the disbanded portions of the Hebrew army; and other fresh volunteers out of Naphtali, Asher, and Manasseh, (vii. 23,) are not slow to join the pursuit. But ever prompt and fruitful in expedient, he remembers that there are hundreds of villages, (containing the most warlike men of Israel,) among these very mountains, at whose feet the routed host had paused. Quick as lightning he summons the Ephraimites to the chase. They were instructed to seize the passes of the Jordan, and prevent the Bedouins from eluding their grasp. For the latter, once across the river, would escape to the wastes of their own deserts, or plunge into thickets and forests, with which they were familiar. As one man, the tribe of Ephraim responds to the summons. They are too late, indeed, to arrest the flight of the two greater kings, Zebah and Zalmunna; but they succeed in intercepting the second great detachment, which is headed by the smaller chieftains, Oreb and Zeeb, at the fords of Beth-barah. The Raven and the Wolf—though swiftness (as implied in both names) may have been their characteristic in retreat as well as in battle—have not been able to evade the sudden dash of the great warrior tribe of Central Palestine. The Ephraimites do not wait instructions from the lips of the commander as to the disposal of the royal captives. In the very spot where they were seized, their heads are cut off. "The Raven" was captured as he mounted a rock, or tried to conceal himself in one of its clefts, and there slain; and it got ever after the name of "the raven's rock"—"the rock Oreb." "The Wolf" was caught—brought to bay—crouching in a wine-press, in a cavity similar to what I described at Ophrah: and there, too, the blood of Zeeb was shed,—the place ever after retaining the name of "the wolf's wine-press." There must, however, here have been a last desperate struggle of these despairing men. The fight seems specially to have raged around the Raven's rock, and the slaughter there to have been most dreadful; for the memorable day and deed were afterwards known and described in connection with that rock as unparalleled. When Isaiah speaks of the utter destruction of the great Sennacherib and his hosts in coming against Jerusalem, he can find no such adequate comparison in Hebrew history, as in the two great victories at Oreb and the Red Sea,—giving even the priority to the former,—"The Lord of hosts shall stir up a scourge for him, according to the *slaughter of Midian at the rock of Oreb:* and as his rod was upon the sea, so shall he lift it up after the manner of Egypt," (Isaiah x. 26.)

Cutting off the heads of the two princes, the

Ephraimites recross the Jordan with their bloody trophies, which they present to Gideon and his exhausted band. In that moment of victory, when all tribal jealousies and complaints should have been forgotten, the haughty Ephraimites cannot resist taunting Gideon with the apparent slight they had received at his hands at not being requested, as a tribe, to take part in the previous battle. If the Hebrew commander had been elated with the pride of triumph, he might have resented the unworthy and unseasonable charge. But with that prudence, and tact, and courtesy, which was one of the characteristics of his noble nature, he appeases their mistimed wrath by flattering their vanity. He points to the slaughtered squadrons below, and with this soft answer turneth away wrath: "What have I done now in comparison of you? Is not the gleaning of the grapes of Ephraim better than the vintage of Abi-ezer?" As if he had said, "Have not you, men of Ephraim, greater glory in coming in at the last and clenching the victory —bringing with you two such bloody trophies —than we, the clan of Abi-ezer, who, though we have had the brunt of the fight, have no such splendid booty to exhibit?" Thus the apparent or intended slight was happily turned. "Their anger toward him was abated when he had said that," (viii. 3.)

But there is no time for dallying or altercation. The two greater chiefs—perhaps with the picked men of the sadly diminished army—have crossed the Jordan, and they may make good their escape if further delay be indulged. Gideon, with his 300, leaving the Ephraimites at the bloody field around Oreb, disappears down the gorge of Jordan, and, crossing one of its fords—probably at Bethshean—gives chase to the retreating horde. "Faint, yet pursuing," is the brief record of his pursuit. Well were his faithful men entitled to feel exhaustion and fatigue. But, as I have explained at the commencement of the story, one of the main objects of the conflict—at all events in the eyes of their leader—has yet to be accomplished, and with unflagging energy they hold on their whirlwind course through Eastern Manasseh, assured of help from on high. The Midianites who had escaped, numbered only 15,000, out of the enormous host of 135,000. These, with their two kings, had halted at a place called Karkor. We have nothing to guide us to the precise locality. Eusebius speaks of it as fifteen miles north of Petra, but it is improbable that it could be so far south as that. But when Gideon and his men overtook the Bedouin remnant, it must have been after a long and forced march, as Josephus speaks of the Midianites pitching their tents "a great way off." Most probably it was to the open desert, on the Hauran, (far removed from built villages or cities,) in their own familiar wastes, that they betook themselves, imagining that they would be there secure from the pursuit of the victors. The only guide to the direction of the route they had followed, is the recorded incident regarding Succoth and Penuel—two names that remind us of earlier Bible scenes in the life of the Patriarch Jacob. At both these places Gideon pauses with his exhausted troop, and demands of the citizens to furnish him with victuals. Succoth came first on the line of pursuit. On reaching its gates, the request was courteously preferred: "Give, I pray you, loaves of bread unto the people that follow me; for they be faint, and I am pursuing after Zebah and Zalmunna, kings of Midian," (viii. 5.) The inhabitants, however, not only churlishly refuse, but seem to cast a slur on those making the demand, by insinuating that they will fail to succeed in their attempted capture. Their crime is more aggravated by far, than that of the men of Meroz, in the pursuit of Barak, who, it will be remembered, in dogged silence shut their gates, but offered no taunt or reproach to the conquerors. The Succoth citizens, in this avowed insult, have bearded the lion in his den. The wonted courtesy of Gideon is changed into stern indignation, and, in the impulse of the moment, he makes the vow—(surely very unworthy of his natural magnanimity, but for which the peculiar circumstances of the case must so far plead palliation)—that on his return he would "tear their flesh with the thorns of the wilderness and with briers," (viii. 7.) Penuel is the next town, on the way, which could afford refreshment for himself and his weary men. As it was situated on a height, their fatigue must have been increased with the ascent. But here, too, it was toil and labour in vain—Gideon fares no better. The citizens of Penuel and the Succothites seem to have come to a mutual understanding, and the latter give him a similar refusal. The pride of their border city was its high watch-tower. He vows, on coming back from his pursuit, to lay it in ashes. Its ruins would be a permanent memorial of their selfishness, visible for miles around. It is not difficult to imagine the reason of this curt refusal by these two unhappy cities. Had they opened their gates and provisioned Gideon's troops, while these, after all, were repulsed, the Midianites would have made cruel reprisals—executed upon them summary retribution. With that intense selfishness which so often rules and regulates the actions of cities and nations, they naturally inferred that 300 weary men would have a poor chance against 15,000 trained soldiers of the most warlike tribe of the East.

These calculations of the two border cities, however, were erroneous. Gideon comes suddenly upon the vanquished remnant. Humanly speaking, had these comparatively fresh Midian soldiers—who must have had hours of repose—braced themselves for the struggle, there could be little doubt as to the result; —faintness and fatigue would, in ordinary circumstances, have had no chance with recruited strength and numbers. But the name of Gideon had become a word of terror. Moreover, from the narrative, he would seem to have fallen upon them either in another night attack or in the early dawn of morning, (viii. 13.) Mounted on the backs of their swift dromedaries, Zeba and Zalmunna made a renewed effort to escape by flight; but the handful of warriors overtook them. All the host was discomfited, and the chieftain captives were conducted back in triumph.

Shortly after daybreak we see the cavalcade

retracing their steps across the desert with their magnificent trophies, and then wending their way through the long defiles leading to the Jordan.

The story of the rout is best and most graphically told, not in the sober words of the narrative in Judges, but by the same future minstrel and hymn-writer of the nation whom we found celebrating the discomfiture of the hosts of Sisera, (Psalm lxxxiii. 13, 14.) It is a vivid picture which is there given of the suddenness, completeness, and terror of this later defeat. Their flight over the uplands of Gilead is compared to the chaff of the threshing-floor, or the dry stubble of the wilderness driven by the hurricane; or to the flames which, in a tropical country, when every blade and bough becomes like tinder, sweep along in wild and furious career, till whole mountain ranges are reddened with the conflagration. Truly the old injunction we have already noted as given to Israel, to "vex Midian and smite them," has been terribly fulfilled.

We are not told of any other Midianite captives,—most probably they were either all slain or put to flight. Gideon reserves alone the two haughty chieftains alive. Seated still on the richly embroidered saddle-cloths on the backs of their dromedaries, Zeba and Zalmunna—the renowned sheikhs who, but a brief week before, had made all Israel tremble —move along in sullen silence. Touching must have been the sight of that gorgeous magnificence and fallen glory. Their very dresses and accoutrements are made familiar to us in the Book of Judges, and help to fill in the picture. Their rich silken abbayehs or cloaks; the still richer kerchiefs which shade their brows and stream gracefully over their shoulders; their pendant collars of massive gold, or set with precious stones; the earrings, and nose jewels, and bracelets. Even the noble animals they ride, and which are alone ignorant of the humiliation, are not forgotten in the original narrative, with their housings of finest crimson, trappings of cloth of gold, the golden bells jingling round their necks and falling on their tufted breasts.

The procession has reached Penuel—the same place where, many ages before, Jacob had seen God face to face—where he wrestled with the angel and prevailed. Here they halt. Gideon, though flushed with victory, and, we might have thought, with blood enough on his hands, has not forgotten the vow of yesterday;—their watch-tower is demolished, and all the men of the city remorselessly put to the sword. The victorious band pass on to Succoth. The conqueror discovers from a young citizen of the town the number and the names of the princes (or heads) and elders,—those who had been responsible for refusing his demand for bread; and with branches of the prickly thorn so common throughout these lands, he executed the threatened vengeance by scourging them to death,—according to the quaint expression in the original Hebrew, "with them he taught the men of Succoth," (viii. 16.) It was a hideous method truly of imparting a memorable lesson on the penalties due to combined cowardice and selfishness. They proceeded on their homeward march. Jordan's fords are re-crossed, and the two kings of Midian, arrayed in their now mock royalty, re-traverse the scenes of the first slaughter. Crossing the plain of Esdraelon, we infer that they have reached Gideon's own highland village and home at Ophrah. The "court-martial" of these olden days was summarily held. The two potentates were brought before the victor. And how does he address them?—what, according to the term of our courts of law, is the *indictment* he brings against them? Is it an accusation of being the marauding chiefs who, at the head of their followers, had for years been the disturbers of Israel —laying waste their plains, and valleys, and hamlets? Is it on account of that long seven years' vassalage which they had compelled his countrymen to suffer, that he pronounces and executes against them a sentence of death? Doubtless, as a righteous judge and true patriot, all these considerations would have their sway. Moreover, none can doubt that the relief of his fatherland would, in the eyes of a truly great man like Gideon, outweigh all personal considerations. Yet, from an expression which he lets slip in the very act of passing sentence, (viii. 19,) his generosity would evidently have spared these vanquished men, if other stronger reasons, I have formerly referred to, had not imperiously demanded the pronouncing of a capital sentence. The first (the only) question he addresses to these representatives of fallen greatness, shews where, during all these days of fierce conflict, his own thoughts mainly were. As already noted, they were on the bloody scene that had been transacted weeks or months before on the top of Tabor, when his brothers' blood has crimsoned its green summit, and left him the terrible legacy and responsibility of being their avenger. "Then said he to Zeba and Zalmunna, What manner of men were they whom ye slew at Tabor?" Though at the risk of repetition, let me remind my young readers that this is the true key to Gideon's persevering and determined energy in following up the victory. After the fearful slaughter at the rock of Oreb, at which the invaders might be said to be annihilated, we fail to see that it would otherwise have been worth his while to push his handful of faint and exhausted troops after the miserable remnant who had escaped to Karkor. He would probably have rested content with the laurels he had won, and sought repose for himself and his men. But the terrible debt which had been brooding all the while in his inmost soul, could only be paid by the blood of those who had slain his mother's children. The brief words which I have just quoted, as he addresses his regal prisoners, leave us no doubt as to what was uppermost in the Goel's mind. "What manner of men were they whom ye slew at Tabor? And they answered, As thou art, so were they; each one resembled the children of a king. And he said, They were my brethren, even the sons of my mother: as the Lord liveth, *if ye had saved them alive, I would not slay you*," (Judges viii. 19.)

These haughty but humbled chieftains know now—indeed, ever since their capture they knew too well—what their fate would be. According to the great Hebrew scholar, Gesenius, the name Zalmunna means, "shelter is denied him." They pre-

THE SLAUGHTER OF ZEBA AND ZALMUNNA.

pare for the worst, and resolve to die as Arab heroes should. Gideon's own son, Jether,—a boy, a lad, —is present at the closing scene. He, too, sustains the same relation with his father to the royal culprits, as avenger of his uncles' blood. Was it to add to their humiliation, that, in the first instance, the boy is asked to lift against them the fatal weapon? We almost would hope better from Gideon's magnanimity;—but whatever was the motive which inspired this first suggestion, the tender child-nature recoils from the bloody task—his hand refuses to lift a weapon in such a cause. This enables the proud victims to prefer the one last request, that if die they must, it may not be with the irresolute thrust or blow of a youth, which would leave them to linger in agony—but by the unerring stroke of the conqueror himself, "Rise thou, and fall upon us: for as the man is, so is his strength," (Judges viii. 21.) Their petition is granted: Gideon's sword stretches the bodies of Zeba and Zalmunna at his feet. *Then*, observe, having thus revenged his brothers' blood, (but not till *then*,) follows the stripping the bodies of the slain, and disrobing the camels of their housings and neck-gear. Never was there a more complete victory! Well might the trumpets of jubilee sound through the land—well might every mountain-top have its joyous beacon! If there had been another Deborah, she would have celebrated, in equally exalted strains, what was left to a prophet of a future age,—the glories of the day, when "broken was the yoke of his burden, and the staff of his shoulder, the rod of the oppressor in the day of Midian"—when there was a joy throughout all the land, "according to the joy in harvest, and as men rejoice when they divide the spoils"—"when the battle" of these warriors of Israel and Midian (from the crashing of the pitchers to the blood-shedding at Ophrah) was "with confused noise, and garments rolled in blood," (Isaiah ix. 3, 4, 5.) No words can better describe the grandeur and thoroughness of the triumph, than those of the sacred record: "Thus was Midian subdued before the children of Israel, so that they lifted up their heads no more," (Judges viii. 28.) Indeed, the awful completeness of it became a proverbial form of expressing the extremity of Divine vengeance on all the kings and great ones of the earth who would range themselves as the enemies of God and His Church:—"Make thou their nobles like Oreb and like Zeeb; yea, all their princes as Zebah and as Zalmunna," (Psalm lxxxiii. 11.) No wonder that a grateful and admiring country wished its hero to accept of royal honours, and to have the first crown of the kingdom of Israel put upon his head. "Then the men of Israel said unto Gideon, Rule thou over us, both thou and thy son, and thy son's son also; for thou hast delivered us from the hand of Midian," (Judges viii. 22.) Gideon modestly refused the profferred dignity. Having nobly done his mighty work, he has no wish for the honours and pageantry of state. He would rather peacefully retire to his native village, and resume the congenial pursuits of agriculture. Besides, he had a nobler motive in thus declining the royal sceptre. By assenting to be sovereign, he felt he would have been usurping the place of a higher. God had proclaimed himself alone to be King of His chosen Israel;—and the loyal, faithful servant of Jehovah will not dare to invade the Divine prerogative. "And Gideon said unto them, I will not rule over you, neither shall my son rule over you: the Lord shall rule over you," (viii. 23.)

In one thing alone did Gideon mar the grandeur of his illustrious triumph. When his brave troops are still around him, covered with the spoils of victory, he makes the request—that from these varied treasures, and specially from the golden earrings of the Ishmaelites, each soldier would give a contribution. They cordially assent. The victor spreads one of the mantles of the disrobed kings on the ground, and into its ample folds there is thrown a mass of earrings alone, which weigh a thousand and seven hundred shekels of gold! With this he makes an ephod, or sacred garment, adorning it with "ornaments, and collars, and chains," (ver. 26.) If, originally, Gideon was impelled to this act by the most sacred of motives—giving a thank-offering or tithe of all he and his people had won to the God of Israel, in acknowledgment of His interposition on their behalf—he did wrong in alienating the worship of the nation from the sanctuary of Shiloh—the appointed place of devotion, where the ark of the covenant was, and transferring these to his own village or town of Ophrah. Another result was what was to be expected,—this jewelled ephod "became a snare to Gideon and his house;" for it came, like the calf of old in Horeb, to be made an object of adoration—and seduced the people into idolatry. With this exception, however, the country enjoyed the blessings of his beneficent judgeship. We can picture to ourselves the renowned hero, gradually merging into the old man, sitting by the gate of Ophrah, and dispensing justice and judgment, not only to his own clan and tribe, but to "all Israel." And from the apostacy from the true God which, immediately after his removal, we are specially told took place, we gather with what piety and wisdom he had wielded the rod of power for a peaceful period of forty years. He thus lived respected and beloved at Ophrah, and died the father of a numerous offspring. The phrase so familiar in old patriarchal times is repeated of him, "he died in a good old age." When the family "sepulchre of Joash his father, in Ophrah of the Abi-ezrites," is opened, we can picture the thousands who, with weeping eyes and funeral dirges, would follow him to his last resting-place. Perhaps the most valuable testimony borne to his work—the most valuable panegyric—is that which, in long after ages, was borne to him by the greatest of Christian apostles. St. Paul puts Gideon first in his roll of heroes; and he expresses his regret that time forbids him enlarging on his character,—"Time would fail me to tell of GIDEON," (Heb. xi.)

Shall we not conclude with a word of fond hope regarding Gideon's old foes, these scattered "Children of the East"—true still to their old Ishmaelite character—their hand against every man, and every man's hand against them. The day is coming, that bright day of the future, so beautifully pictured by the very prophet who speaks of the day of Midian, with its confused noise and blood-stained garments, —when amid the multitudes coming to "the brightness of the Saviour's rising," will be included "the *dromedaries of Midian*,"—no longer carrying their militant chiefs, their weapons of war, and their hoards of plunder; but on a nobler, diviner errand, —"they shall bring gold and incense; and they shall shew forth the praises of the Lord," (Isaiah lx. 3, 6.)

IV.

STORY OF JEPHTHAH.

THE next Warrior-Judge who claims our attention is one with whom a sad and pathetic tale is associated, which has given his name a melancholy interest which it would not otherwise have possessed. Jephthah of Gilead—or the Gileadite—is put upon the illustrious roll of titled heroes—along with Gideon, Naaman, and others—as "a mighty man of valour."

It was still considerably more than a thousand years before the Christian era, when the battle of Aroer, which we are about to describe, was fought, and in which Jephthah was the leader of the army of Israel. Before proceeding, however, to an account of this new war, and its sad sequel, it will be interesting to know something of the commander's birthplace, and his previous life.

The home of his family and tribe was on the eastern side of the river Jordan, that tract of country with which we have become partially acquainted in our last, in describing Gideon's pursuit of the retreating hordes of Midian. If not so well known as the western portion of Palestine, the land of Gilead was by far the more varied and picturesque of the two. Its simplest geographical boundaries, as given by a modern writer, are, from the south-eastern extremity of the Lake of Tiberias on the north, extending south, with the Jordan as its western frontier, to the northern end of the Dead Sea. In extent it is about sixty miles in length, and not more than twenty broad, (Dr. Smith, *Bible Dictionary*, *Art.* "*Gilead.*") On the east it merges into the sandy wastes of Arabia. It is a region connected with many memorable passages in Hebrew history. Abraham crossed its uplands and wild forests in his journey from Mesopotamia; Moses, from one of the peaks of its Pisgah range, got a full view of the land he was forbidden to enter; David made it the place of his exile when driven from his throne by the treachery of Absalom; the great Elijah came forth from its mysterious seclusion to brave the apostate sovereign of Israel and the thousands on Carmel. Nor are its associations confined to Old Testament times. At the opening of the Christian era, the feet of our blessed Redeemer trod its mountains and valleys. There is a strong probability that these formed the scene of His temptation, rather than the portion of the wilderness of Judah which tradition has long pointed out as such. It was the region to which the sisters of Lazarus, in the hour of their bitter sorrow, sent the messenger with the tidings, "Lord, he whom thou lovest is sick," and towards which they strained their eager gaze impatient for His coming. Finally, on the crests of one of its mountains was situated the city of Pella, whither the Christians—remembering the words of the Lord Jesus—had fled, when the flames were mounting over the doomed city of Jerusalem.* Travellers who have had courage to brave the roving Bedouin hordes that now scour that entire country, describe its varied natural beauty. Long stretches of green pastoral "downs," varied with valleys clothed with olive and fig, oak and terebinth. Some deep glens intersect it, hurrying their spring and winter torrents to the Jordan.

* See all these various incidents in connection with the Transjordanic region described by Dr. Stanley, in his *Sinai and Palestine*, p. 317-328.

Among these, specially, are the two rocky gorges of the Jabbok and the Arnon; while among the smaller ravines we may most probably include the brook Cherith, where the Tishbite prophet was fed by the ravens during the famine in Samaria. However great the desolation may be which has now passed over it, it must at one period have been a most productive soil, yielding a singular variety of fruits and grain. When one of its aged chiefs—Barzillai the Gileadite—with his brother chieftains, came to offer sympathy to the exiled king of Judah, they brought the following substantial offering of its products: "Wheat, and barley, and flour, and parched corn, and beans, and lentiles, and parched pulse, and honey, and butter, and sheep, and cheese of kine," (2 Sam. xvii. 27-29.)

If such was of old the richness of the land of Gilead in general—the land of balm, gums, and spices, and aromatic herbs—there is perhaps no single point in the region so remarkable in historical interest as what is called by pre-eminence *the* "Mount Gilead." What the Mount of Olives was to the south, or what Hermon was to the north, this mountain—though of vastly smaller elevation than the latter, and dwarfed, too, in effect by the hills around it—was, nevertheless, the 'Jebel-sheikh,' the kingly summit, to the inhabitants of Eastern Palestine. Although it had the advantage in height over the adjoining eminences, its celebrity arose mainly from the sacred recollections attached to it. On its top Jacob and Laban erected their heap of stones as the joint witness of the sacred covenant into which they had entered on parting. That cairn, or possibly the watch-tower which may have subsequently enclosed it—"Mizpeh of Gilead"—must have been visible from afar. Indeed, the whole mountain would assume proportions in the distant view, (and especially from the Eastern desert,) which were a good deal lost on a nearer approach; for we read that Jacob, on that same occasion, after crossing the river, (Euphrates,) "set his face towards *Mount Gilead*," as if it had formed a conspicuous landmark for the Syrian caravan. It is worthy of note, too, in passing, that while this same occurrence in the life of the Patriarch and his father-in-law gave the name alike to the mountain and to the whole district, it was the Gentile from Mesopotamia, not the grandson of Abraham, who suggested that name. It was Laban who said, "This heap is a witness between me and thee this day; therefore was the place of it called 'Gal-eed,'" (which means "the heap of witness.") It still retains to this hour, among the tribes who pitch their tents at its base, the appellation, "Jebel Jil-ad"—Mount Gilead.

We have given this description of a mountain less known than others in sacred story, because there are strong grounds for supposing that it was here [Mizpeh of Gilead—with its ancient fortress or 'keep'—the "look-out"] that the Warrior-Judge of this story had his early home;—that it was here he assembled his army, and from it proceeded on the march we are shortly to narrate. "The spot," says a writer already referred to, "is admirably adapted for a gathering-place in time of invasion or aggressive war." Wild rugged mountainous territories have frequently been the nursing-place for heroes. In our two previous stories, the elect champions were found amid the hills of Naphtali and Manasseh; while the same has been illustrated in a more striking form, in different ages, amid the mountains of Thessaly in Greece, the Apennines in Italy, the Grampians of Scotland, the Alps of Switzerland and the Tyrol. It was so, apparently, also in the case of a country which could produce, among others, two such characters as Elijah and Jephthah. Nay, it was as the 'military tribeship' that Gilead was selected by warlike Manasseh, when Joshua was partitioning the land; for we are expressly told regarding Machir, the elder born son of Manasseh, "*because he was a man of war, therefore* he had Gilead and Bashan," (Joshua xvii. 1.) Gad, one of the other tribes who held this martial region, had the following appropriate description given of him from the lips of dying Jacob: "Of Gad, a troop shall overcome (or plunder) him: but he shall overcome (plunder) at the last." He was to be the Ishmael of the Hebrew people;—every man's hand was, in one sense, to be against him. This arose from the position of his territory in its relation to the rest of Palestine: it had always to bear the first brunt of attacks from eastern invaders. Yet victory was finally assured to him.* It is one of these "troops" we are now to speak of—as "overcoming;" but, by the valour of a new chieftain, the plunderers are to be repelled, and independence re-asserted. Jephthah is about to anticipate the victorious war-song,—the hymn of thanksgiving sung in after years by the son of Jesse,—"Gilead is mine," (Psalm lx. 7.)

It is the old story which ushers in this new war. The Hebrews had relapsed into idolatry. This relapse, I fear, extended to the whole nation, but it specially applied to the eastern tribes in the region

* See on all this the *Art.* "*Gilead,*" in Dr. Smith's *Bible Dictionary.*

just described. What did more than anything else in their case to foster the tendency, was their proximity to the heathen and superstitious kingdoms around them; for, we read, "The children of Israel did evil again in the sight of the Lord, and served Baalim, and Ashtaroth, and the gods of Syria, and the gods of Zidon, and the gods of Moab, and the gods of the children of Ammon, and the gods of the Philistines, and forsook the Lord, and served not Him," (Judges x. 6.) We need not wonder at the sequel. According to the strong language of the narrative, "the anger of the Lord was hot against Israel, and He sold them into the hands . . . of the children of Ammon." For the long period of eighteen years this warlike nation—with whom, in former times, the Hebrews had been confederate against the gigantic Og of Bashan—vexed and oppressed them in turn. Nor were the Ammonites content with subjecting the Gileadites alone to this vassalage. They pushed their armies across the gorge of Jordan, and overran the mountains of Ephraim and Benjamin, and the cities of Judah. This long and grievous servitude produced its most salutary result in a national mourning and penitence,—"The children of Israel cried unto the Lord, saying, We have sinned against thee, both because we have forsaken our God, and also served Baalim," (x. 10.) Their guilt, however, at this advanced period of their history, after all the lessons they had formerly been taught, but taught in vain, had its great aggravations. The Almighty Being they had provoked refuses at first to listen to the nation's cry, seeing that former similar humiliations had often only ended in a return to idolatry. The suppliants are therefore at first repelled with the righteous taunt, "Go and cry unto the gods which ye have chosen; let them deliver you in the time of your tribulation." Another, and still deeper wail of penitence bursts from the lips of the people, accompanied with the destruction of their idols and images. Great must that terror have been, when it is spoken of as "the misery of Israel," (x. 16.) But the cry is heard—they are to receive "of the Lord's hand double for all their sins."

The armies of Ammon seem to have been massed in the land of Gilead. The well-known horn of Israel, whose blast we have found summoning them before to Tabor and Gilboa, brought them now to the central mountain and sanctuary of the trans-Jordanic tribe. We are not told the numbers of the resolute defenders. But we gather, that, on their part, there was no lack of patriotism. The military tribe, true to its warlike instincts and prestige, had not to be accused of apathy and cowardice, such as we noted in both the former campaigns of the west. "People and princes" had responded to the call. One difficulty—one great blank alone are they conscious of, without which valour, and daring, and numbers can be of little avail. They are without a competent and reliable leader. Is there no hero similar to Barak or Gideon that can be found to head their armies, and lead them to victory? If they but knew of any such, equal to the momentous task, they would reward his services with what would be equivalent to a crown—they would rally around him as their future chief, and load him with grateful honours.

There *was* one, and only one, that could be thought of. But there were hindrances in the way of his acceptance which might be insuperable. "A mighty man of valour" was that JEPHTHAH. To no one, under God, could they better entrust their fortunes. They could safely confide in his skill, and prudence, and desperate courage. But, then, the likelihood was he would resent such an offer. He had a stain on his birth for which he had cruelly suffered at the hands of his own family. He had been thrust out of his father's house by jealous brothers, and, in terror of his life, he had fled to the wild woods in "the land of Tob." Perhaps his own bravery, and the unmerited slur and insult that had been cast on him, had been well known, and created among those who loved a wandering existence a sympathy for the outcast and outlawed man. Be this as it may, that secluded forest which he had made his own abode was turned into the resort and rendezvous of freebooters. Jephthah's wild roving life, at this time, reminds us of that of David amid the caves and fastnesses of southern Judah before ascending the throne; or, if we can make so sudden a transition to a very different age and country, and borrow a familiar name and example from English history, he became the Robin Hood of Gilead. Far in these forests and pastoral "downs," amid wandering herds of cattle and troops of lawless men, he seems, according to Josephus, to have held a sort of mimic court. He was the acknowledged head of this band of adventurers, and led the existence of a roving Bedouin. A procession of venerable men, deputed by the assembled army at Gideon, are seen one day approaching the robbers' haunt. He receives them, and listens to the proposal they bear—viz., that he would leave his desultory warfare and bandit life, and come and be the leader of the expedition against the armies of Ammon. They promise, at the same time, that, if successful, they would confer upon him permanent dignity as their head—their chief, and 'Warrior-Judge.' His wounded honour causes him at first to hesitate; but, on second thoughts, he assents, on the express understanding that, if the army of Israel should prove victorious, they would faithfully fulfil their promise, by elevating him to the highest honours. They repeated their stipulation; upon which he, and probably his lawless mercenaries, struck their forest tents, and proceeded forthwith to Mizpeh, where the army was mustered. There, on being installed as chief captain or commander at its sanctuary, (would it be by the 'heap of stones' at the watch-tower which crowned the hill?) he took care to have the aforesaid covenant between himself and the elders rehearsed and ratified.

The armies are now both prepared for battle. Previous, however, to engaging in the fight, negotiations are exchanged between the chiefs:—these were perhaps begun on the part of Jephthah with the view of obtaining time;—possibly, too, from the desire this rough freebooter had to save needless bloodshed, if the long quarrel can be otherwise settled amicably. I shall not enter into these messages and counter-messages—the charges that were made, and how they were repelled. As is the case with all wars, both sides had evidently old grudges to settle, and old wounds to heal. 'What right have you Ammonites to come on our territory?' said Jephthah. 'What right had you Israelites to rob me of these territories when you came through the wilderness from Egypt?' retorted the King of Ammon. 'They are my patrimony,' said Gilead. 'They were mine long before,' replied Ammon. And so on the altercation went, with a number of geographical details and respective claims introduced into it, with which we need not cumber and complicate the story. In one word—the King of Ammon sought and demanded a rectification of frontiers:—but this rectification amounted to nothing short of restoring the whole district from the Arnon to the Jabbok, with the Jordan as the western boundary. This, of course, Israel stoutly refused. The warlike feelings became further intensified by the introduction of the religious element. The Hebrews recognised the hand of Jehovah in the dispossession, (ver. 23;) while they hurled back the taunt, "Let thy god Chemosh get it back if he can," (ver. 24.) In the protest of their elect chief the quarrel is thus summed up: "Wherefore I have not sinned against thee, but thou doest me wrong to war against me: the Lord the Judge be judge this day between the children of Israel and the children of Ammon. Howbeit the king of the children of Ammon hearkened not unto the words of Jephthah which he sent him." Negotiations having ceased, there is nothing remaining but (to use a modern phrase) the fearful arbitrament of the sword. In the words of Josephus, the Israelitish commander "sent the ambassadors away, and prayed for victory."

"The Spirit of the Lord came upon Jephthah." He was "clothed" (as in the case of Barak and Gideon) with new strength and Divine qualifications for the onerous post he held.

But this brings us to the mournful incident of the story:—the interest surrounding Jephthah and his army is now transferred to another and new actor in the tragic scene.

It was a custom among Pagan nations of old—as it is a custom among savage tribes still—to propitiate their deities by human sacrifice. Jephthah, we have every reason to believe, was a worshipper of the true God of Israel. Though not an inhabitant of Palestine proper, (or at all events living on the other side of the Jordan,) he was, nevertheless, an Hebrew of the Hebrews—a genuine son of Abraham—nay, one of the illustrious heroes whose name, by the great Apostle, is held up for our admiration—as having "*by faith* subdued kingdoms, waxed valiant in fight, and turned to flight the armies of the aliens," (Heb. xi. 32.) At the same time it could hardly be expected that he could altogether escape the evil influences of the idolatries, and demon-worship, and superstitious practices which prevailed around. In other places in Scripture, we have evidence that this most unnatural of rites was by no means uncommon among the nations bordering on Gilead. Let one example suffice. In the long subsequent reign of Jehoram and Jehoshaphat—when these two kings, confederate with Edom, marched against the Moabites—the King of Moab, in the extremity of revenge and despair, took the heir-apparent of Edom, and on the wall of his only remaining city, "offered him for a burnt-offering;"—evidently with the wild hope that a life so precious might propitiate his tutelary deities, and save his own crown, (2 Kings iii. 27.)

When we bear in mind that Jephthah—'of the stock of Abraham'—had in his possession, in common with his tribe, a written law, in which the practice of human immolation was rigidly prohibited, it may seem, indeed, strange, that he could have been so contaminated with the creed of these votaries of bloodthirsty Moloch, as to suppose that the most frightful part of their orgies could be in any wise acceptable to the Jehovah of their fathers. It must be remembered, however, that, from various causes, the people, and more especially those of the trans-Jordanic tribes, were living in great ignorance of the Levitical statutes, whether as regarded their requirements or prohibitions. Though Shiloh, the place of the sanctuary and the abode of the High Priest, was, geographically, not far distant, yet, not only did the deep gorge of Jordan very much sever the eastern tribes from intercourse with the western, but what rendered any such intercourse at the present time well-nigh impracticable, was the breach that had taken place between Ephraim and Gilead. Even in obeying one of the most stringent of their requirements—going up at the Feast of Tabernacles, to hear the law read once every seven years at the appointed place of celebration—few would dare to brave the animosities of a high-spirited and vindictive race like the Ephraimites; and, for the same reason, the High Priest, who would naturally be resorted to for consultation in seasons and questions of difficulty, was, for the present, virtually beyond reach. Jephthah's religious views were, accordingly, in many respects crude and imperfect; and, among the other superstitions of the neighbouring nations, he had not escaped the influence of their revolting ideas on the subject of human sacrifice. It has been suggested that perhaps one of the oldest and most memorable incidents in the first settlement of his race in Canaan, might, to a distorted vision like his, seem to plead some justification for the dark purposes that were brooding in his mind, and which have left a cruel blot on his otherwise noble name and deeds—I refer to the commanded immolation of his own son by the father and founder of the Jewish people, on the top of Mount Moriah; a deed, too, which would have been accomplished, but for the intervention of Jehovah's angel. Be this as it may, when Jephthah is now on the eve of marching to the field of battle, he makes the secret vow, that should the arms of Israel prove successful,—on his triumphant return, the first living being who should meet his eye, would be offered in sacrifice as a burnt-offering and thank-offering to the God of the Hebrews. It may be well to give the very words of his rash covenant:—"And Jephthah vowed a vow unto the Lord, and said, If thou shalt without fail deliver the children of Ammon into mine hands, then it shall be, that whatsoever cometh forth of the doors of my house to meet me, when I return in peace from the children of Ammon, shall surely be the Lord's, and I will offer it up for a burnt-offering," (Judges xi. 30, 31.)

The vow is registered in heaven, and in the hero's heart, and soon his warlike mission is accomplished. We have no details of the fight. Whether stratagem, as in Gideon's case, had to be resorted to, in order to produce a general panic before the battle —or whether, as is more probable, a rapid march was followed up by a desperate assault—and this again by the total rout of the enemy, we cannot tell. All we are informed is, that the slaughter was "very great,"—that the battle which raged at Aroer was continued in a long and bloody pursuit "even to Minnith,"—and that no less than twenty of the "giant cities" of Ammon fell into the conqueror's hands.

And now comes the homeward march. The tidings of the triumph have preceded the conqueror to his native city. Among the many rejoicing hearts in Mizpeh, there was one pre-eminently so, who mingled the exultation and gladness of an Israelite with the pride of a daughter. Her father, by his personal valour and skill as leader of the armies of Gilead, had wiped off the stain which had been cruelly affixed to his earlier life. He had won the gratitude of an admiring country. What else, what less can she do, when the rest of the city are preparing for him an ovation, than to deck herself in her festal attire, and from the parental roof, like the mother of Sisera on the latticed turret of Harosheth, watch his approach, that she may go forth, cymbal in hand, to give her loving welcome. The sound of martial music falls on her ear, telling that the glad moment has arrived, when she may rush into his arms, and, with a daughter's caresses, congratulate him on his victory. We may imagine, too, what the father's thoughts would be. It is the proudest of moments—that of the hero returning triumphant from the fight. A Hebrew conqueror, as much as a Roman on his way to the Capitol, would require the slave by the side of his chariot to whisper the monition in his ears,—"Remember thou art mortal." Among Jephthah's other high and glowing anticipations would doubtless be, that the future promised honours would be shared by one dearer to him than life—

the child who alone bore his name, and could transmit it to posterity. As he approached through these upland valleys nearer and nearer his home, could he not, however, possibly at times be haunted with the horrible misgiving, that she who was the light of his dwelling might be the owner of the unhappy life that was about to be forfeited in the payment of his vow? But no! he dismisses the repugnant thought. The walls of Mizpeh are in sight—its gates are flung open. He is on his way to his own residence. Alas! the little ewe lamb of the future prophet, unconsciously leads herself, arrayed in festal fillets, to the slaughter. His eye falls on the first figure of a bright procession, approaching with music, and dance, and song, from the steps of his threshold. But—oh misery of miseries!—his saddest fears are realized; it is, indeed, as is emphasized in the narrative, "his only child: beside her he had neither son nor daughter." The wretched father, smitten and broken-hearted at the sight, tears his garments—those garments which were probably decked with ornaments and trophies of victory—and utters the piercing cry, bringing the revelation of the awful secret, "Alas, O my daughter! thou hast brought me very low, . . . for I have opened my mouth unto the

Lord, and I cannot go back." The brief narration leaves us only to picture the agonies of these moments which cannot be described. The fond parent finds that he has sold to remorseless death the pride of his heart and of his life; and what is worse, he himself must be the murderer! She is the first to break the dreadful silence, or rather, she is the first to increase the poignancy of his grief by the manifestation of a hero-spirit worthy of his own name and fame, and worthy of a better cause,—"My father," she said,—(and must not that opening word have been as an arrow to his sensitive soul,)—"if thou hast opened thy mouth unto the Lord, do to me according to that which hath proceeded out of thy mouth; forasmuch as the Lord hath taken vengeance for thee of thine enemies, even of the children of Ammon." Brave patriot! so willing to lay herself on the altar of her country;—a young life so full of bud and early blossom, with the brightest and proudest of futures before it. But she manifests no shrinking—she ventures on no remonstrance;—there is something passing noble in her chivalrous indifference to the unnatural doom. She has lived to see her father victorious and her country free; and if their joint thanksgivings are to find utterance in the pouring out of her young blood on the altar of Mizpeh—it is enough. Let them gather the fire and the wood —she is ready to be "the lamb for the burnt-offering."

And well she knew—well also did the stricken father know—that "having opened his mouth, he dared not draw back." The Levitical law was explicit: "Every *devoted* thing is most holy unto the Lord. None devoted, which shall be devoted of men, shall be redeemed; but shall surely be put to death," (Lev. xxvii. 28, 29.)

The sentence may, however, for a few weeks be deferred; and it is her only pleading and request that, for two months, in company with her youthful companions, she may absent herself from the household, and wander about among the rugged ravines and mountains around, bewailing the disappointed hopes of her young and tender life. They were the same scenes among which the future minstrel of Judah, in later years, gave vent to some of his most plaintive Psalms. The request is granted. More to be pitied even than the doomed victim is the wretched parent, whose lip, in a rash and unguarded moment, had uttered the vow. How sadly and slowly to him would these long mournful hours roll by, until the morning came, when, probably with no eye dry or

"O Israel, thy hills are resounding,
The cheeks of thy warriors are pale,
For the trumpets of battle are sounding,
Both matron and maiden do wail."

heart unmoved amid the thousands that congregated around, the fearful stroke descended. The tragic scene is not described. On some altar, possibly erected by the door of the dwelling where the eye of the returning father had first greeted her, or, possibly, on the mountain summit at the ancestral sanctuary—the piercing cry of one who was mourning for an only child, and "in bitterness for a first-born," would go up amid blood and flame. It has been well said, the writer would seem as if he wished to hurry over as soon as possible the last details;—the veil is drawn over the end with the brief words, "He did with her according to the vow which he had vowed," (xi. 39.) What to him would be all the glories of that bloody field of Aroer, with the spoil of its twenty cities! The oldest meaning attached to his Gilead home could never be realized in his own case and that of the lost one, on this side of death—"'Mizpeh,' for he said, The Lord watch between me and thee, when we are absent one from another," (Genesis xxxi. 49.) All that remained in his now voiceless, desolate hearth, was the memory of her heroic goodness—the two jewels in her martyr crown—filial obedience and filial love.

The touching story, as is well known, has been a favourite theme with many poets. The great musician Handel has also seized upon it, and weaved it into one of his grandest oratorios. Nothing in sacred song, indeed, can be more touching or plaintive than what he has set in music to words supposed to be uttered by the anguished father,—the horror of the contemplated deed beautifully melting into the strains supposed to be sung just when the spirit has fled—strains in which he commits the soul of his darling into the keeping of the waiting angels who had just borne her to heaven:—

"Deeper and deeper still, thy goodness, child,
Pierceth a father's bleeding heart, and checks
The cruel sentence on my faltering tongue.
Oh, let me whisper it to the raging winds
Or howling deserts. For the ears of men
It is too shocking! Yet, have I not vowed?
And can I think the great Jehovah sleeps,
Like Chemosh, and such fabled deities?
Ah no! Heaven heard my thoughts, and wrote them down.
It must be so—'tis this that racks my brain,
And pours into my breast a thousand pangs,
That lash me into madness. Horrid thought—
My only daughter! and so dear a child,
Doomed by a father. Yes, the vow is past,
And Gilead hath triumphed o'er his foes.
Therefore to-morrow's dawn . . . I can no more.

Waft her, angels, through the skies,
Far above yon azure plain,
Glorious there like you to rise,
There like you for ever reign!"

The only remaining incident in the story, is the statement of the writer in Judges, that that sad sacrifice was made, ever after, the occasion of a sacred anniversary. The daughters of Israel (possibly the young Gilead maidens alone) set apart four whole days each year, on which they assembled beside some rocky cave at Mizpeh which held the dust of Jephthah's daughter, to lament her untimely fate—to perpetuate the remembrance of her rare devotion to duty, and, as she doubtless thought, to God.

Some writers have attempted, in various ways, to explain away the reality of the hideous story altogether, by endeavouring to take a figurative view of the narrative. Among other explanations, for example, it is held that, instead of so unnatural and revolting a human sacrifice, no more is intended but that Jephthah shut up his daughter in a separate house during the remainder of her life, and that the maidens of Israel were permitted, for four days every year, to visit the solitary, and condole with her in her forced seclusion. We agree with the brief verdict of a well known and able writer on Jewish history, that "All these expedients are far more improbable than that a fierce freebooter, in a period of anarchy, should mistake an act of cruel superstition for an act of religion," (Dean Milman's *History of the Jews.*)

Jephthah, though several years of mental grief were still before him, had not leisure, immediately after the awful tragedy, to brood over his sorrows. The war with Ammon was closed, but the swords of his soldiers had other work in store for them before they would be sheathed: although, alas! in the present instance, the collision arose from a bitter quarrel, not with Ishmaelites and Bedouins, but with one of their brother tribes. You will remember how haughtily the proud overbearing Ephraimites resented Gideon's accidental or intentional oversight of them in the Midianite war, and how it was only by a courteous and conciliatory answer that he averted more angry words and more vengeful deeds. Some similar feeling of wounded dignity had anew roused the injured susceptibilities of the same tribe. "They gathered themselves together and marched northward," for the purpose of taunting Jephthah because he had not invoked their assistance to share with him the glory and the spoils of the battle of Aroer. They threatened a species of vengeance, which seems to have been not an uncommon way of expressing Oriental indignation—viz., to burn his dwelling-house, and to include himself in the conflagration. Jephthah does not seem to have had the policy to soften down their wrath, as Gideon did, by throwing a sop to their vanity. He denied the truth of the accusation they had laid to his charge, and produced further irritation by charging them with apathy, inasmuch as their assistance had been sought, but no response was made to the appeal. A pitched battle was the result of these recriminations. It was the painful spectacle of one of those tribal or internecine wars which so often cursed the future of Palestine. We know not the exact spot where the conflict took place. It is evident, however, that the incensed Ephraimites had been the aggressors. They had crossed the river Jordan, invading the soil of Gilead. Gilead, under the conduct of Jephthah, was victorious, driving the army of the other tribe down the ravine to one of the river's fords or passages—very possibly the same which had formed the scene of slaughter in "the day of Midian." By some dexterous manœuvre, or by a forced march, the Gileadites reached the Jordan before the retreating Ephraimites. There seems to have been considerable confusion, and this was increased in consequence of the similarity in appearance, dress, and language of the foes. Though the latter was in both cases the same, the dialect was different. As in our own country, the words used in one shire or district often cannot be accurately pronounced by those living in another,—or to take another apposite illustration, as the *th* of the English cannot be pronounced by a German,—so a Gileadite would be able to detect an Ephraimite from a halting lisp, or from the slurring over of a consonant. Such was the strange expedient to which Jephthah resorted, in order to distinguish between his own men and those of his enemy. He took a *pass-word.* The word selected was *Shibboleth*, ("water-flood,") the same word that is used in the 69th Psalm, 15th verse: "Let not a *shibboleth* of waters drown me." It was repeated without difficulty by all the men of Gilead. But when the escaped Ephraimites, to evade the fury of the foe, attempted to exercise deception, and to pass themselves off as Gileadites, they were commanded to utter the testing word. If they failed to pronounce the second consonant, they were condemned by their own lips, and put to the sword. "Then said they unto him, Say now *Shibboleth;* and he said *Sibboleth:* for he could not frame to pronounce it right. Then they took him, and slew him at the passages of the Jordan," (Judges xii. 6.) What between the battle and the Jordan 'passages,' there was a slaughter of the Ephraimites of 42,000.

After this, Jephthah, so far as either civil or foreign wars were concerned, seems to have spent the remaining six years of his life and of his Judgeship in peace. There is a strange contrast between the closing years of our last Warrior-Judge, Gideon, with his enormous family, and those of the childless chieftain of Gilead. The latter may have lived (let us trust he did) to entertain juster views of the character of Jehovah than that He required, like the Ammonite Moloch, to be propitiated with human blood. And yet, did views and feelings truer to the deepest instincts of humanity thus return, what an awakening they must have brought along with them to a sense of the rashness and guilt of his vow! It would be like the thrilling account Williams, the great missionary to the South Sea Islands, gives of the agony and torture of mind endured by the converts to Christianity, when they began to reckon up, as fathers and mothers, the number of helpless children they had, in the blindness of heathenism, immolated to their false deities, and all of whom might have had their still living lips attuned to the praise of a God of love, who desireth not sacrifice.

Nor can we forget that Jephthah's awful oblation, and the tender victim's devout submission, form the nearest possible human type of the one *Great* Offering—the one Great "Propitiation for our sins; and not for ours only, but also for the sins of the whole world,"—when, in answer to the question, "Whom shall I send, and who will go for us?" the answer of Divine filial obedience and filial love was made, "Behold, here am I; send me!" "Lo, I come: I delight to do thy will, O God!" "He was oppressed, and He was afflicted, yet He opened not His mouth: He is brought as a lamb to the slaughter, and as a sheep before her shearers is dumb, so He openeth not His mouth," (Isaiah liii. 7.) "God so loved the world, that He gave *His only begotten Son*," (John iii. 16.)

V.

STORY OF SAMSON.

THE last, properly speaking, of the Warrior-judges is different from all his predecessors. SAMSON has been generally, and with truth, regarded as the most singular and eccentric character in Scripture. We almost seem at times, indeed, in reading his history,—so full of wayward, unregulated impulse,—to feel as if we were out of the sacred region altogether, and had wandered unknowingly among the wild legends of Eastern romance, where heroism and cruelty, levity, frolic, and sin, are strangely commingled. There is nothing of true nobleness—nothing of the nobleness of Gideon—about him. His greatness mainly consisted in the lower qualities of muscular strength and feats of prodigious personal daring. In these he had no parallel. But we confess to disappointment, after the angelic agency which, as we shall presently see, was employed at the intimation of his birth, that the promised champion, of whom so much was expected, turns out to have so little that appeals to the higher emotions and sympathies of humanity, and so much that is wild, erratic, mischievous, corrupt. He seems to be one in whose character there were the elements of much that was commendable. If he had been wisely guided, or rather, had he wisely guided himself, he would have lived to be a great and a good man. But he abused his gifts and endowments: qualities which, had they been properly directed, would have given him a place among the most illustrious of the Hebrew race, were degraded and perverted to minister to folly, and selfishness, and vice. If our book had been "Tales of the Hebrew '*Worthies*,'" instead of the Hebrew "*Judges*," we could scarcely have given Samson a place in that gallery of moral heroes. His picture, or rather the many and varied pictures his life supplies, are far from being in harmony with other portraits of pure colouring which surround him in holy writ—Abraham and Moses, Joseph and Joshua, Samuel and Eli, Elijah and Elisha. He never was, or could be, looked up to with the confidence and respect which these inspired. Even had his prowess been more fruitful in results than it was, it is not likely that, as in the case of Gideon, he would ever have been solicited by the nation to become its regal head.

And yet, we dare not overlook traits in him which served to qualify and redeem those that were earthly, and sensual, and devilish. Among these, he was full of good humour, mirthful, frolicsome. His name, which signifies "Sunlight," was appropriately bestowed. His jokes, and riddles, and merriment, must have carried sunshine and sparkle with them wherever he went, and perhaps tended, and were designed in their way to wake up to hopefulness and fresh life the cowed and broken spirit of the nation. More than this, we discover now and then a simple, child-like trust in God. Perhaps, too, we have not had revealed to us the best lights in the picture of his life. We fondly cling to the hope and belief, that the young faith, nurtured by his pious parents, returned at the close of his fitful career,—that as often with his prototype in the firmament after a day of darkness and cloud, so with this "sunlike" man, may there not have been rays of goodness, gleams of nobleness, that came out in the murky evening of his life, which amply warranted the great Apostle, in his chapter on faith and its examples, to include the playful and erratic giant of Dan? There are spots on the natural sun, and no character in this world can claim perfection. With every deduction which the many grievous faults in his character constrain us to make, he was, notwithstanding, the Hero of his tribe and his age; and his exploits have had a fascination to all young Bible readers, shared, perhaps, by no other character of the sacred record.

In another respect, as we shall find, Samson differed from the Warrior-Judges who preceded him. He was never engaged in conducting any great campaign—heading an army against Canaanites, or Midianites, or Ammonites, as in the case of Barak, and Gideon, and Jephthah. His are all feats of personal valour. He is in himself the army of Israel. The Philistines are on one side, and Samson, his own individual self, is their antagonist. The scene of the struggle, too, is limited: and this brings me, before entering specially on Samson's successive exploits, to say a few preliminary words on the history of that great and powerful tribe with which he was so often brought into conflict, and which, indeed, long after his death, continued the most stubborn of all his country's enemies.

In our two last stories we have spoken of the Midianites and Ammonites of the far East—the wild freebooters from the Arabian wilderness. Our thoughts are now directed to the opposite side of Palestine, to the fertile expanse of land immediately north of the desert of Egypt, with the Mediterranean on the west, and the hills of Judah its eastern boundary. The Philistines—the "strangers" or "foreigners," as the word means—are generally supposed to have been originally a colony from Crete. They were a pastoral tribe who had emigrated from this isle of the Great Sea previous to the time of Abraham. It is supposed that a second emigration had taken place from the same island about the time of which we now write. When the Hebrews entered the land of promise, at the close of their wilderness wanderings, the primitive settlement of the aliens had grown into a powerful and wealthy nation. This was not difficult to account for. Of all portions of Palestine, this border settlement was the most productive. Corn-fields, interspersed with olive gardens and vineyards, spread, almost without a break, on its rich soil. The district has been well described as "a little Egypt." In seasons of famine and scarcity, when in other parts of the land there was no fruit in the vine; when the labour of the olive failed, and the fields supplied no meat; the famishing population—just as their ancestors had gone to the unfailing banks of the Nile—"went down" to this granary of the nation. The Phœnicians deemed it their greatest prize at the time of a later conquest; and even at this day, when desolation reigns in other parts of Palestine which were formerly fertile,—rich crops, vineyards, olive-forests, and orange-groves stretch from its old northern boundary at Joppa to the ancient Ekron. The vast plains I speak of were occasionally broken by gentle elevations. On these the Philistines had built their five principal cities, Gaza, Askelon, Ashdod, Gath, and Ekron. Two of these were maritime. Gaza and Askelon had their navy as well as their vessels of commerce, for we read of the former encountering the war-ships of Rameses III. of Egypt. The same would appear to have been the trading capital, or mart. We are told of the stores of frankincense and myrrh captured, among other treasures, by Alexander the Great, (Dr. Smith's *Bible Dictionary*, *Art.* "*Philistia.*") Gaza, indeed, could hardly fail to be important as an emporium of merchandise; for the land of Philistia and the way of Gaza by the south, formed the route by which caravans passed to and from Phœnicia and

Egypt. The inhabitants of this border territory were, many of them,—like the Rephaim of Moab, of whom we formerly spoke,—of gigantic stature. They were greatly in advance of their neighbours, the Israelites, in the appliances of war. Their smiths and armourers are made special mention of. It has been well observed, that "the most complete vocabulary of armour which the Bible contains, is taken from the panoply of a Philistine warrior—Goliath of Gath," (Dr. Stanley.) Like the Canaanites under Jabin, they had a vast advantage over the mountaineers of Israel in their well-appointed chariots. The flat plains of Philistia, like those of Esdraelon, were well adapted for their use in battle. Their raids and plunderings remind us of "the Children of the East" in Gideon's time. Stealing at midnight from their fenced cities through the pathways intersecting their corn-fields, they made frequent and sudden attacks on the unsuspecting highlanders of South Palestine, pillaging their barns and threshing-floors. The Philistines in another respect resembled the Midianites, in the abject terror their frequent forays had inspired among the villagers to the east of their territory. So great had been the panic, that the ordinary roads were closed; the inhabitants skulked by night and by stealth along bypaths; the very wells, with their precious contents, were rendered inaccessible. Many fled for refuge among the limestone caverns in which Southern Judah abound; while not a few who had preferred braving the fury of their invaders, were captured and sold as slaves. The Philistines had taken the most effectual method to disarm their rivals, by shutting up their foundries, and smiths' shops, and arsenals, thus preventing them fabricating instruments of war. If we come afterwards to read of 600 men of the Danites armed with weapons, it must be borne in mind that this occurs after Samson had rallied the broken spirits of his countrymen, and subsequently also to his own death, (Judges xviii. 11.) It must be acknowledged that the Israelites, thus crushed and dispirited, had become all the easier a prey to their neighbours, on account of their own unfortunate divisions and tribal jealousies. The Philistines, on the other hand, had proved that union is strength; for while their five cities were in one sense independent, and ruled each by its own chief, they were confederate in their hostility to the new settlers, and acted in concert, to repel Israelite aggression. This was one of the secrets of their continued sway in the Holy Land after the rest of the old inhabitants were conquered. Of all the foes of the Hebrew people, their name carried with it the greatest dread. Such hold, indeed, had the presence and rule of the Philistine taken, that even after their long dominion had ceased by the conquest of David, the entire country retained the name of its long oppressors—Philistine, or Palestine.

At the time of which we now write, this vassalage had continued for the space of forty years. But though Israel, and especially the neighbouring tribes of Dan and Judah, seemed almost to have resigned themselves to an unworthy despair, there were ever and anon some brave exceptions to the general cowardice—heroic spirits who attempted, if not to throw off the yoke, at all events to inflict retribution on their ruthless spoilers. Among these was Shamgar, the son of Anath. He was a contemporary of Deborah's; one, doubtless, of the many sufferers who had been roused by repeated wrongs to take a savage vengeance on his country's foe. Heading his clan of peasant followers, he sallied forth on one memorable occasion, and, with the most primitive of weapons, in the absence of better, slew with "ox goads" 600 men. But far greater than Shamgar is the Hero whose strange story we are about to tell. The story itself occupies many chapters of the sacred narrative. I shall endeavour to bring before my readers its most salient and interesting incidents.

It was the smallest of the twelve tribes that was to give birth to the last of the Warrior-Judges. To the tribe of Dan—("the Judge")—that rich region of Sharon and Philistia, which I have just described, was assigned by Joshua on the partition of the land. We cannot wonder that the Philistine settlers keenly disputed the right of the new comers to possess the luxuriant soil, and that they made every effort to coop them up amid their mountain fastnesses. The Danites, on the other hand, could only look down from their hill fortresses with vain and ineffectual longings on the valuable prize which was still wrested from their grasp. But they were now to have a champion given to them, whose deeds would go far to rally the coward spirit of the whole nation. The name of his birthplace is Zorah. If it is the same which has been visited and identified by Dr. Robinson, it lies on the slope of a sharp-pointed conical hill, about two hours' distance direct west from Bethlehem, and overlooking that vast extent of plain, more than once referred to, otherwise called the '*Shefelah*,' or low country. The same traveller, who visited the spot in the season of spring, speaks in glowing terms of the noble fountain situated beneath the village as "gushing" with water; a term that can seldom be employed with reference to the streams of modern Palestine. "As we passed on," says he, "we overtook no less than twelve women, toiling upwards, each with her jar of water on her head. The village, the fountain, the fields, the mountain, the females bearing water, —all transported us back to ancient times, when, in all probability, the mother of Samson often, in like manner, visited the fountain and toiled homeward with her jar of water."

In the fortress city, or fortified camp of the tribe—Mahaneh-Dan, (probably the fort adjoining Zorah,)—lived Manoah and his wife: the latter is spoken of by Josephus as being a Jewess of great beauty. A Divine visitant, "whose countenance was as the countenance of an angel of God, very terrible," (Judges xiii. 6,) appeared to her, with the announcement that she was to bear a son. He added special directions as to the manner of his bringing up. From his cradle he was to be consecrated to Jehovah. As a double proof and pledge of this consecration, no razor was ever to come upon his head,—his locks, in other words, were never to be shorn;—and though surrounded with the fruitful vineyards of Timnath and Zorah, his lips were never to touch their purple clusters. He was to drink no wine—he was to be a Nazarite unto God from his birth. The visit of the angel was repeated a second time in the open field. The wife of the villager was here seated alone,—probably brooding over her strange destiny, as about to be the mother of one whom she, her tribe, and the whole nation of Israel had, for half a century, ardently longed, until hope deferred had made the heart sick—a deliverer from the Philistines. Manoah also listened to a repetition of former injunctions from the lips of the visitor; and failing at first to recognise his angelic nature, he proffered (as was the wont of Orientals) the rites of hospitality, and expressed his purpose of preparing a kid for the meal. The mysterious messenger refused the offer, suggesting rather that it should form a "burnt-offering to the Lord." The Angel also declined to gratify Manoah's curiosity by the revelation of his Name—that, he said, was "Mystery," or "Secret." But the wondering pair were left with no doubt as to his lofty nature; for on the slain animal being laid on the adjoining rock, and there consumed by fire as a burnt-offering, the august Messenger was borne away to the heaven from which he came, on the cloud and flame of the sacrifice, and was seen no more.

The whole opening transaction leaves us with the impression, that these two Israelites were "Israelites indeed,' filled with faith and piety, and that the child about to be born would be the child of many prayers. On the birth taking place, the infant received the name of 'Samson.' In accordance with the command of the heavenly messenger, he was duly consecrated and set apart as a Nazarite. It is well known that there were many religious "fraternities" instituted in later times in the Christian Church, beginning with those of the early centuries, and extending to the Franciscans and Dominicans of the Middle Ages. The Nazarites formed the only "ascetic order" we know of under the Old Testament dispensation; (and even that name can only be given them in a qualified sense.) Their rules were not so rigid and exclusive, by any means, as those of the anchorites and monks of a subsequent era. Regarding abstinence from strong drink the injunctions were most stringent. They were not only forbidden to taste wine, but, to prevent any possible evasion, the very stones and skin of the grape were mentioned among the things proscribed. Equally rigid was the prohibition to cut the hair of the head. According to the Mishna —so particular were they to ensure the carrying out of this to the letter, that though Nazarites were allowed the use of a brush, they were forbidden that of a comb, as more likely to lead to an involuntary infringement of the vow;—while females guilty of departure from the oath were liable in punishment to forty stripes. The only other prohibition was the coming in contact with a dead body. Even that of a parent was forbidden to be touched. We are told of Helena, the queen of Adiabene, that although she completed a voluntary Nazarite vow of many years, to secure the success of her son's arms,—yet, in consequence of touching a corpse just at the expiry of the time, she had to undergo an additional seven years before she could be released from her obligation. This latter requirement, however, could not always have been obligatory. Certainly not so, at all events, in the case of Samson, who, as we shall find, must have been brought at one time, by his own prowess, in contact with the bodies of a thousand slain. The only "Nazarites for life" with whom we are acquainted in the early Church, were John the Baptist and St. James the Just. Eusebius informs us regarding the latter, that he was consecrated from his birth neither to eat meat, to drink wine, to cut his hair, nor to use the bath. St. Paul's is an example of the minor Nazarite vow—which continued in force for a limited number of days, in acknowledgment of some special token of the Divine goodness, or of deliverance from danger.

Such, then, is a general description of the order of Nazarites, or "separated ones," of which Samson was the most notable example in Old Testament story. His bushy unshorn head—the seven long curls which streamed from his giant shoulders, must have given a wild savage look to the champion. Well might Milton speak of "his illustrious and sunny locks,"—"his puissant hair" "waving about his god-like shoulders."* And if to this we add, as has been conjectured, that the Nazarites wore a peculiar garment, whether of regal purple or rough camel's hair—he must have grown up a marked man in his native city. Josephus interprets his name as "the Strong." It was, at all events, appropriate—strong in unexampled muscular power, with these strange twisting symbols, peculiar to him, of a diviner strength.

Of his childhood and boyhood we know little or nothing. The whole notice of this period of his

* See quotation in Dr. Stanley's *Lectures on the Jewish Church.*

life in the sacred record is: "The child grew, and the Lord blessed him;" followed by the further intimation, that "the Spirit of the Lord began to move him at times in the camp of Dan, between Zorah and Eshtaol. We are left in imagination to picture the young elect hero, the pride of his youthful comrades and companions, giving indications of his future character by his feats of strength, his frolic and merriment, and, it is not too much to add, his roguish pranks. Wherever the ringing laugh would be heard loudest in the streets of Zorah, among the young citizens, Samson would be there with his burly form, and shaggy locks, and sunny countenance. He and they would perhaps, from time to time, indulge their freaks in mimic warfare against the dwellers in the distant corn-fields, whom they had been trained to regard as the bitterest foes of their country; and their leader would begin, in the playfulness of boyish plots, what he afterwards consummated in successful stratagem. This "lion-like youth" would doubtless have the consciousness in his more sedate and sober moments—(this increasing as his age advanced)—that the God of his nation was nurturing him for momentous deeds. His pious parents would often refresh his memory with the great destiny in store for him,—reminding him of the signal honour which had preceded his birth, by an angel having been expressly sent from heaven with the prophetic commission and announcement, "he shall begin to deliver Israel out of the hand of the Philistines." By the expression "the Spirit of God began to move him," we must certainly infer that he was gifted with supernatural powers. The Spirit of Jehovah began to "strike, as the expression implies, on his rough nature, as on a drum or cymbal, till it resounded like a gong through his native hills," (Dr. Stanley's *Lectures*, p. 367.) It is somewhat remarkable, as the same writer observes, that "the names of the surrounding villages bear traces of the wild animals which he afterwards encountered, and used as instruments of his great exploits,—Lebaoth, ('the lioness,') Shaalbim, ('the jackals,') and Zorah, ('the hornets')."

His first exploit refers, not to a war tale, but to a love story. The future hero, when probably on the threshold of youthful manhood, was strolling one day amid the vineyards of Timnath, or Timnathah. The village of that name probably corresponds with the modern *Tibneh*. If so, it is perched on the slope of the hills of Dan, which we have already described as melting into the rich maritime plain of

Philistia. It must have had a commanding situation, as it was selected long after, in the time of the Maccabees, for one of the fortified posts of Judah. It was then on the border of the Philistine territory, but near enough the Judean mountains and forests to be the haunt, as we shall immediately find, of various wild animals.

Either in the streets of this border town, or among the vintage-gatherers on the neighbouring slopes, the eye of Samson was captivated by one of the daughters of the Philistines. In eager haste he retraces his steps to his native village, and acquaints his father and mother with his desire to obtain her for his wife. We can readily imagine the distress and disapproval with which such an announcement would be received by his parents,—that one whose future had been so specially foreshadowed as the conqueror of the Philistines, should desire thus foolishly to entangle himself in an unseemly alliance with one of their females. They attempted remonstrance;—but perhaps they already knew too well the rash and impetuous nature of their son, to be convinced that their expostulations would be ineffectual. Samson displays no great filial reverence or courtesy on the occasion, for he cuts the remonstrance short by the somewhat imperious reply, "Get her for me, for she pleaseth me well." As the narrative indicates, however,—that like the marriage of Isaac and Rebecca—"the thing proceedeth from the Lord." This marriage connection, otherwise unfortunate and unhappy, was to be overruled as the means by which the champion was to deal his first blow at the oppressors.

In accordance with Eastern custom, the father and mother, waiving with reluctance their scruples, set out along with their son, from their home on the mountains, to arrange his betrothal with the Philistine maiden. On their way thither, Samson digressed from the footpath among the vineyards around Timnath. A young lion was couching among the vines, and, by his savage growls, gave evidence that he was about to dispute the right of the young giant to intrude on his domain. It may be noted in passing, that, as is the case with other wild animals mentioned in Scripture, the lion at present is not found in Palestine. The nearest lairs of this "king of the forest" are said to be in the southern desert, on the way to Egypt; or, more numerous still, among the jungles around the banks of the Euphrates and Tigris. In former times, however, the lion seems to have been no stranger in the land of Israel. As has just been indicated, the name of a village close to the scene of Samson's exploits, is associated in some way with the lioness and her cubs. Lions are spoken of as coming up from "the swellings of Jordan;"—the inundations of the river driving them from the tangled thickets of reed and oleander, and the caves in the limestone banks, where they had their dens and covert. The youthful David's encounter is well known to all; and Beniah, one of his body-guards, distinguished himself by slaying one of these animals in a pit of snow. It must be remembered that Palestine, in ancient times, and especially the mountainous region around Zorah and Timnath, now barren and treeless, was covered with dense forests of terebinth and olive, which gave harbour to many beasts of prey which are now extirpated. It was no imaginary sound described by the great Psalmist of the nation in his beautiful hymn on creation and providence, but one which he had himself doubtless often heard, when wandering amid the forests and gorges of Engedi and Hareth—"The young lions roar after their prey, and seek their meat from God," (Psalm civ. 21.) His royal son was possibly speaking also from personal knowledge, when he refers, in his Song of songs, to "the lions' dens," and "the mountains of the leopards," (Song of Sol. iv. 8.)

It was one of these young, but full-grown lions, that was now couching among the vines of Timnath, lashing his sides with his tail in fury, and about to spring on the adventurous Israelite. "The Spirit of the Lord," we read, "came mightily upon him." He was nerved and endowed with fresh physical strength; and, with no weapon to parry the assault save his own brawny arms, he tore his assailant in pieces, as the fabled Hercules did the Nemæan lion, as if he had rent a tender kid of the goats. The mangled animal lay dead at his side. In the words of Josephus, "he strangled him with his hands, and cast the wild beast into a woody piece of ground on the inside of the road." Could he who ventured, so soon after, to make a riddle out of the occurrence, fail to take home the lesson and encouragement from this first deed of heroism, that in the same manner would the lion-like strength of his country's foes be rent in sunder? If such thoughts, however, suggested themselves, they are, for the present at least, locked in his own bosom. Another errand is now occupying his mind, and on issuing from the daring fray to join his parents, he resolves not even to mention to them his encounter. He might be afraid, perhaps, that in pointing the above moral, they might be encouraged to make another attempt to dissuade him from forming so undesirable a marriage connection. Timnath is reached. He and they have an interview with the Philistine damsel. The customary betrothal took place, and the preliminary arrangements being settled between the respective parents of the youthful pair, Samson, with his father and mother, returned to their home in Dan.

The time of betrothal, which generally extended over some months, having expired, Manoah, his wife, and son, are again on the same journey, in order to have the nuptials completed. They are once more approaching through the old vineyard to Timnath. The youth, full of pranks as ever, and nothing loath to have, perchance, another tussel with a tawny monarch, again strolls from his parents at the spot of his former encounter to see if he could find any remains of the carcass. There it is. The meat and bones, the flesh, and, perhaps, even the skeleton, are clean picked and consumed by the ants, vultures, and other insects and birds of prey, who make short work in these countries with carrion. The hide alone remained. But it was not alone; for, during the interval, it had become a haunt of busy life, and a hoard of food. If, as we have said, the lion was at one time common in Palestine, much more so was the bee;—so common, indeed, that, as is well known, the distinguishing feature of the country was "a land flowing with milk and honey." The bee found a receptacle for its labours in the crevices of the rocks, in the hollows, and even the thick branches of the trees—as when Jonathan found honey dropping in the wood, (1 Samuel xiv. 26.) It was used as an article of ordinary food at the Jewish meals. A swarm of these busy workers had settled in this strangest of hives—the lion's carcass, and made it the receptacle of their store. The young hero takes away in his hand a portion of the honey, and his parents share with him in tasting it; although, on this occasion too, he is reticent as before, as to how or whence, in this playful digression into the vineyard, he had procured the honey. But the little incident was treasured in the mind of the jovial and humorous youth, and would be turned to use in due time, when occasion offered.

They have again arrived at Timnath, and the protracted marriage ceremonies begin. These consisted very specially in a feast, which extended over the long period of seven days—"exactly the same period as the feast with which, six hundred years before, Jacob celebrated his successive marriages,"

(Dr. Kitto.) At this part of the festive ceremony the customs of the Orientals differed, and still differ, widely from ours. The feast was not given by the parents or friends of the bride, but by the bridegroom. Moreover, it was contrary to Eastern etiquette for the bride herself to be present at this lengthened entertainment. The bridegroom was responsible for inviting his and her friends, called in the Gospels "the children of the bridechamber," (Matt. ix. 15.) In the present instance these amounted to the number of thirty. The wedding-feast of Samson also explains and illustrates other customs connected with that auspicious time, elsewhere referred to in Scripture. The bridegroom, for example, was released from the irksome and onerous duty of attending personally to the wants of his guests. His "groomsman," called "the friend of the bridegroom," or, at the marriage at Cana, "the governor of the feast," dispensed the rites of hospitality, (John ii. 8.) He was 'president' or 'chairman,' and is called in the Bible narrative of Samson's feast, "his companion, whom he had used as his friend," (xiv. 20.) We have strong reason to suspect that the greater number of the thirty guests at these Timnath nuptials, possibly most of them self-invited, were Philistines, who had their own clandestine designs upon their unsuspecting host.

A seven days' feast, ungraced and unenlivened by female society, even though it were the marriage entertainment of a radiant, sunny soul like Samson, must have been a slow and wearisome affair. The mere coarse enjoyment of eating and drinking would soon end in surfeit; topics would run out, and conversation lag; and some expedient was, on all such occasions, necessary to change the monotony and help to while away the time. It was the custom, accordingly, for the guests to amuse themselves by propounding puzzles or riddles. This, indeed, has always been a favourite pastime with Orientals. We have it on the authority of Josephus, that even King Solomon did not deem it beneath his dignity, or higher intellectual resources, to engage in the solution of riddles with his brother king of Phœnicia. Samson was, of all men, best fitted for taking part in such humorous enigmas, and he proceeds to enliven his banquet and kill the time by propounding one of these. From the proposal with which he accompanies it, it will be a riddle, too, worth pondering and solving; for should any one of the company succeed in interpreting it, each of the thirty guests would receive a forfeit from himself;

—that forfeit would consist, in all, of thirty linen dresses, and thirty richer robes. While, on the other hand, if they failed in the solution, he would exact from his guests a corresponding one. The proposal evidently meets with cordial approbation; and in that mingled company of Philistine and Israelite, we can imagine the dull oppressors, who formed the majority, and the fewer but more quick-witted oppressed, bending forwards to catch the strong man's words. "Put forth thy riddle," they all exclaimed, "that we may hear it." The riddle was as follows, in Samson's own words:—"Out of the eater came forth meat, and out of the strong came forth sweetness." They spent three days of unavailing effort over this perplexing problem. It was too evident they had no clue to its solution. The guests, however, and especially the Philistine portion of them, were not to be outwitted by the knowing bridegroom. If not by fair, then by clandestine means they must get the explanation. Not only must they succeed in being themselves acquitted from the charge of dull incapacity, but, in their mercenary calculations, they must escape so serious a forfeit, and secure the valuable reversion. There is one ignoble method, by resorting to which they feel they can secretly gain their object, and they do not scruple to resort to it. The young bride will be the most efficient instrument to employ in this piece of artful diplomacy. She will be able, by her blandishments, to extract the secret from her affianced husband in a way that no other can. They threaten her with the severest penalties in case of refusal—nothing short, indeed, of setting fire to her father's house in Timnath, and burning herself and the household in the flames. It was a mean and unworthy action, and a still more barbarous threat. If the young bride had been of the same stuff as the heroic and chivalrous daughter of Jephthah, she would have braved the cruel vengeance rather than have stooped to dishonour. She assents, however, apparently without much demur, to the proposal.

Characteristic is the scene between the young lovers. The bride knows the power of tears. She comes, weeping, to her too pliable husband, and upbraids him with his want of affection:—she charges him that he had ventured to propound a riddle, and had not made her an exception in revealing the clue to it. She tells him, that if he truly loved her, he never would have withheld the solution. In vain he pleads, that not even his own father and mother have had the secret confided to them,—and it must be borne in mind that "the parents always continued to enjoy the first place in the confidence of the Oriental, taking the precedence both of husband and wife," (Kitto.) Her tears flow afresh. For seven whole days she damps the joy of the feast with her taunts, and weeping, and pleadings: "She lay sore upon him." At last his patience and good-nature had to give way. Doubtless little dreaming that she would act the part of betrayer and informant—he unfolds the strange, mysterious story about the carcass of the young lion, and the lodgment of bees with their honey. It is an ill-starred commencement to their wedded life. She goes forthwith, and reveals all "to the children of her people." The feast is now drawing to a close. It is the seventh day of it; and unless the riddle be expounded before the sun goes down, the bridegroom will claim his valuable forfeit. But the guests have gained their purpose. Thus they give the solution to the long perplexing puzzle,—"What," said they, "is sweeter than honey? and what is stronger than a lion?" The discomfited giant chafes under the defeat. It must have been with the iron entering into his soul that he listens to their interpretation: it reveals the faithless artifice of one who had just pledged her troth to him on the marriage altar;—"And he said unto them, If ye had not ploughed with my heifer, ye had not found out my riddle." We can hardly wonder that the lion of his nature was roused to its full fury; although it must also be owned that the severity of his revenge was out of all proportion to the offence. He chafes at the thought that they had succeeded by base perfidy in exacting from him the stipulated forfeit. He will pay it—but it will be at an expense these merry-making guests, and especially the Philistine portion of them, had not dreamt of. He hurries away, single-handed, to one of the Philistine strongholds at Askelon, seizes thirty of the citizens, and after putting them to death, plunders them of their garments, and with these wages of iniquity pays the debt. Having done so, he turns his back on Timnath, with its memory of baseness and fraud, and hastens up the hills to his father's house. Perhaps he acted prudently by abstaining from coming within reach of his treacherous partner, and putting a needful restraint on his own fiery nature; for, had he returned to Timnath, the chances are he might have been tempted to follow Gideon's example, when with the thorns of the wilderness and briers "he taught the men of Succoth," (Judges viii. 16.) We need not be surprised at finding the chapter closing with the statement, that a separation had taken place between him and this Philistine woman, who had proved herself unworthy of the name of wife. We have, moreover, additional evidence that Samson had been fortunate in escaping from the debased company into which he had been thrown at Timnath, when we find that even his chief friend and confidential adviser, "the governor of the feast," was almost immediately united in marriage to the false-hearted betrayer.

After a short period had elapsed, during which his resentment was allowed time to subside, the old kindlier feelings of the hero seem to have returned towards the woman who had so abused his confidence and affection. It is evident that he was unaware of the fact just stated, that she had crowned her former faithlessness by being married to another. In the simplicity of his heart we see him setting out to Timnath with a kid slung across his shoulder, probably to be presented to her as a token of reconciliation and forgiveness. His anger, however, as we may believe, is beyond bounds when he learns that she has thus consummated her base desertion by so speedily transferring her affections. He knew too well that she must have been instigated to her treachery by the Philistines—the foes of his country:

and not so much upon her as upon them he resolves, therefore, to let his vengeance fall. It will be in a shape, too, they will not soon forget. The whole story of his retaliation is in keeping with Samson's character. As we have already noted, there is something comic and out of the ordinary run in all his doings, and the present instance is an illustration. Ehud's weapon, the sword—or Jael's, the tent-peg—or Gideon's, the lash, are too common-place for him. Even in his gloomy moods of vindictiveness and malevolence there must mingle a spice of fun and merriment. The jovial jester and punster at the feast must have his eccentric way too of "teaching the men of Timnath." It is a piece of wanton cruelty, as well as of wanton destruction. When he looks down from the heights of Zorah upon the great corn-fields in the plains below, now fast ripening for harvest, the temptation is too strong not to lay them waste either with fire or sword. The Philistines have grievously wronged him in pillaging and desolating his own domestic hearth. He will, in return, make many homesteads roofless, and granaries empty. He forms the resolution to fire the whole standing crops; and as he cannot expect, in so dastardly a purpose, to call down miraculous flames from heaven, his ingenuity leads him to invent a plan absurd in its novelty, and objectionable on the one ground, had there been no other, that it involved the suffering of innocent animals. There is no apparent reason why he might not, like Gideon and his armour-bearer, have stolen down at night with a goodly band from Zorah, bearing in their hands, like the heroes of the north, pitchers and lanterns, and at a given signal have broken the former, and with the flaming brands have set the corn-crops on fire. But the method he resolved to adopt, in addition to the merit of originality, would ensure wholesale destruction as effectually as if he had employed the services of a thousand men;—while the very meanness of the instrumentality would produce the greater humiliation among his foes. Whether aided, or with his own hand alone, we cannot say, but, among the woods, thickets, and vineyards around, Samson succeeded in capturing no less than three hundred foxes, or, rather, jackals; a species of animal with which the country at all times abounded. Being gregarious—in other words, being found in large droves, they could easily, by means of nets or pitfalls, be secured, so that the number need not astonish us. These jackals he was resolved to make the executioners of his vengeance. With a mischief and cruelty certainly inexcusable in one of the nation's champions, he tied the long hairy tails of two together, "putting a fire-brand in the midst between two tails." Descending, probably in the dark, with these strangest of plunderers to the edge of the corn-fields, the brands were lighted. In a moment the frantic animals, maddened with the cruel pain, rushed wildly along, carrying fire and destruction in their eccentric path. We can imagine Samson (like another Nero looking down on the burning of Rome) watching from some elevation in Zorah the movements of his four-footed incendiaries, —indulging in the merriment of his comical nature at the success of his ludicrous plan, as he saw the strange circles of fire,—now and then a brighter blaze rising, indicating that a "shock," or "olive-yard," or "vineyard," had succumbed to the flames. We may imagine, too, how wide these circles would spread. Had it been in our country, the ravages of the flaming brands would have been confined within walls or hedge-rows. But these plains were one vast expanse, without fence or enclosure of any kind. As was to be expected, the Philistine owners were in dire consternation. The toil of a whole season, in the case of the standing corn, would be gone—in that of the olive-yards and vineyards, the labour and loss of many years. "Who hath done this?" was the enraged demand uttered by the roused inhabitants in the darkness of night. There could be but one reply—"Samson, the son-in-law of the Timnite; because he had taken his wife, and given her to his companion." An act of savage vengeance is the result. In the present instance, however, the punishment was better deserved. The men of the plains, in the blindness of their rage, wreak their indignation on the weak and debased woman who, indirectly, had been the cause of their calamity. Samson's faithless wife and her guilty and designing father are dragged forth, and, in the spirit of the stern law, "an eye for an eye and a tooth for a tooth," the same fiery element which had reduced their fertile fields to ashes, is applied to them:—they are burnt to death.

Still the miserable story of revenge goes on. Very possibly, in the present instance, the Philistines had tried to complete the retaliation by seizing also on the person of the Danite giant. But, with his enormous strength, "he smote them hip and thigh with a great slaughter," (xv. 8.)

After this new humiliation, he retires, like a victorious hero, to "the rock Etam," a natural stronghold somewhere on the south-west of Bethlehem, probably close to the Wady Urtâs,—which afterwards became the gardens of Solomon. There, in one of the numerous clefts or caverns with which these mountains abound, he took up his abode. As he was there within the borders of the tribe of Judah, and within Israelitish territory, he naturally concluded that he was safe from his Philistine foes. He has, however, miscalculated. They are speedily on his track, in search of their victim. As the common enemy of Israel, what an opportunity would this have been for the men of Judah, with the accredited champion at their head, to have struck a final blow at the alien power! But it shews more impressively than words can describe, how the valour, alike of the greatest of the tribes, and of the entire nation, had departed—that, rather than draw the sword, they ignominiously agreed to deliver up the hero of Dan, who had confidingly sought refuge, as he had thought, on friendly territory. 3000 soldiers of Judah make their appearance on the top of the precipice where he has lodged himself—not with the proposal, "Come, lead us on to certain victory:—your name and valour, along with our 3000 swords, and the certainty of our ranks being swollen by other allies, will succeed in driving the long-hated neighbours from our covenant territory,"—but with the unworthy demand of cowards,

"We are come to bind thee, that we may deliver thee into the hand of the Philistines." The very baseness of the proposal seems to have unmanned, for the moment, the champion himself. At all events he feels himself helpless, and can only, in that moment of disaster, couple his personal surrender with the stipulation, that they themselves will not be his murderers. He seemed to recoil from the unnatural doom of having his blood shed by the hands of brother Israelites. They accorded to his request, at the same time securing his strong hands with two new hempen cords, and leading him captive, to deliver him into the power of the Philistines. With what savage exultation would his old enemies see him conducted along, thus firmly bound and handcuffed! Their triumph is already won, and perhaps couriers have already been despatched to "tell it in Gath, and publish it in the streets of Askelon." Their taunts and bitter scorn, however, roused the muzzled lion. With a lion's strength, the Spirit of the Lord coming upon him—he snapped the tight cords "as flax that was burnt with fire." His unloosed hands snatch up the first rude weapon in sight. It happens to be the jaw-bone of an ass recently dead. Otherwise without arms, he rushes —a giant refreshed—on the astonished troops; and before they can retreat from the valleys of Judah, he has slain a thousand of them with his own hand. It is not stated, but we are left to infer a general panic alike of the men of Judah and Philistia, and the hero is left alone to sing his own strange song of victory. That short song gives us another glimpse into the merriness and light-heartedness of his nature. An hour before, he is a doomed, fettered captive, subjected to ignominy—the victim of unworthy cowardice—with almost certain death and torture before him. Now, even in singing his pæan, he cannot resist a humorous allusion, derived from the identity of the two words in the original, which mean "ass" and "mass," (or heap.)

"With the jaw-bone of an *ass* I have slain *masses* upon *masses*,
With the jaw-bone of an *ass* I have slain an *ox*-load of men."

The song is finished; the jaw-bone is cast away; and the name of this singular battle-field is called "Ramath-lehi"—"the hill of the jaw-bone."

It is not to be wondered at, that after a feat of such unparalleled physical strength, the champion should feel exhausted with thirst. Acknowledging devoutly the Divine hand in the present signal deliverance, he calls upon the Lord to satisfy his fainting spirit with a refreshing draught of water.

The God he trusted and acknowledged rewards his faith, either by opening a cleft in the rock immediately overhead, or causing the refreshing fountain to bubble up at his feet. It is added, "When he had drunk, his spirit came again, and he revived." Like all other memorable spots associated with great men and miraculous deeds, it received the name of "En-hak-kore,"—although modern travellers have failed as yet to identify the precise spot. From a hint in Josephus it may have been one of the abundant fountains in that particular district, from which the gardens and pleasure-grounds of Solomon were afterwards fed, (See *Art.* "*Etam*," Dr. Smith's *Dictionary.*) It is pleasant to close this new chapter in Samson's history with an incident which bears ample testimony to his piety, and that, too, in the hour of elation, when we might expect the proud spirit would have been most apt to forget its dependence on a greater than itself.

After this occurrence, a long gap or interval seems to have taken place in the hero's history, during which no great feat of prowess is achieved worthy of being recorded. His heroism seemed to have gained for him the confidence of the nation; and though the Philistines still held their ground within their old territory, Samson was installed as

Judge among the other tribes of Israel, for the period of twenty years.

But the stormy scenes of his later life now begin; —although, speaking of his 'later' years, we must not imagine him an aged man, in the decline of life. His earlier exploits took place when he was in the bloom of youthful manhood, so that now he could not have been past his prime. In these last chapters of his biography, it is the old story which rings its changes in the case of so many characters in sacred Scripture—sin, followed by suffering and retribution.

The scene of the new incidents is not in his own village, or even within the territory of his tribe, but in the principal Philistine city of Gaza;—a city which is almost as old as Hebron and Damascus, and which, like them, continues in existence still. Its ancient importance, independent of its commanding natural situation, crowning an extensive ridge, arose from its being the last frontier town of the south, through which the caravans from Phenicia and Damascus went and came from Egypt, as they do with their more limited exchange of goods at this day. The Ethiopian eunuch, in apostolic times, availed himself of "the way that goeth down unto Gaza," as the nearest and best route from Jerusalem to his distant home near the sources of the Nile. A writer (Van de Velde) appropriately calls it "the key of the country." The best evidence of its strength, as a fortified town, in ancient times is, that it defied the armies of Alexander the Great, with all his engines of war, for five months. Other invaders of Palestine have encamped either without or within its gates, attesting the importance of its conquest. Dr. Thomson, in his "*Land and the Book*," describes the fertile corn-fields which still, as in the days of the Philistines, encircle the modern "Ghuzzeh." These are interspersed with vineyards, almond trees, orange gardens, scarlet-flowered pomegranates, olives, and groves of palm;—while the secret of such tropical luxuriance may be traced to the abundant fountains around this inland city with its still crowded population.

From his native hills and his seat of judgment, three thousand years ago, the Danite hero repaired to this busy capital. There is no light thrown in the history as to the special object he had in thus exposing himself in a city where his name and fame were well known. Despite of the giants which their own territory produced, he would be too readily recognised by the inhabitants, alike from his prodigious dimensions, and from what would more readliy discover him—the long tresses which flowed over his athletic shoulders. Forgetful of the lesson which, twenty years before, he had been taught as to the peril of forming any connection with a daughter of the Philistines,—forgetful of what he owed to himself, his tribe, and, above all, to the distinguished official position he held as Judge of Israel, he went and lodged with a profligate woman of the city. The fact of the great enemy of their country living in their midst, who had in former years humbled them and shed the blood of their sons, opened the old wounds which had so far been healed, and led the citizens to the resolution of taking his life. Their plot is laid. The principal gate of the city, as is the universal custom in Eastern towns, was closed at sunset. They set a guard all night close by, that so soon as it was opened in the morning, and should Samson attempt to retreat by it, they might be ready to arrest him, and put him to the sword. He has, however, been apprised of the stratagem, and "the caged lion" resolves, if possible, to defeat the plot, trusting to his old gigantic strength to do so. At midnight he rose, and stole unobserved to the gate. The troop on guard, little dreaming of his appearance at such a time, had probably resigned themselves to slumber. Besides, the gate itself being strongly barred, they would feel that it was unnecessary, until morning light, to keep vigilant watch, egress being impossible. With a prodigious effort, akin to that which signalized former exploits, he pulled up the gates from their sockets, snapping their apparently secure locks, bolts, and fastenings, and poising them on his shoulders—"posts, bar, and all,"—the great athlete, like another fabled Atlas, bears them along. According to Josephus, he never pauses "until he carried them to the mountain that is over Hebron, and there laid them down." Even in this new adventure we discover the ingenious delight which his strange nature had in outwitting and befooling his foes. It is possible he might quite as easily have waited till morning light, and from some lurking-place close by, with a weapon more powerful than a jawbone, have disabled the sentinels, and unbarred the portal to make good his exit. No, he will rather turn the counsels of the Gaza Ahithophels into foolishness, and pique himself on the clever trick by which he could outdo his enemies, and overturn their calculations. We can even imagine the giant, as he strode onward groaning under his burden, indulging in one of his own peals of laughter on the blank discomfiture of the night-watch, when they awoke from their sleep and found themselves pacing in front of a gateless entrance.

One sin leads on to another. Samson had, in a guilty moment, wandered from home and duty, and thrown himself into the embraces of an abandoned female citizen of Gaza. One fatal plunge having been taken, he prepares for another. In the valley of Sorek—probably not far distant from the city, and famous, as the name implies, for its vines—lived another artful woman of the name of Delilah, well named "the Traitress." Samson, as in previous instances, forgot the only true heroism of purity and virtue, and surrendered himself again to debasing influences. The voice of this charmer only too surely and successfully lured him to destruction. The tidings were soon made known to the five lords of the five Philistine cities, that their old foe had made his haunt the house of this guilty enchantress, and, through her means, they determine once more (and they feel, in the present instance, with greater success) to compass his ruin, —each chief of the five cities offering her the tempting bribe of 1100 pieces of silver—supposed in all to be equivalent to about £600 of our money. They resolve, through her coaxing, to ascertain the secret of his enormous strength. They feel assured there must be some charm, or talisman, or magical art, which gave him so immense an advantage over their own athletic race. Moreover, if they can only, by the blandishments of this woman, get him to unlock the important secret, his demon-power would be at an end. We need hardly rehearse the particulars of the well-known story. The insidious woman fondled him with her caresses, and entreated him, for the love he bore her, to allow her curiosity to be gratified by giving her the key to his colossal physical energy. Samson's playful sportive nature cannot brook restraint, and he begins, unsuspiciously, to toy with his tempter. First, he evasively tells her to bind him with seven green withs or saplings, —probably either the tendrils of some of the vines close at hand, (whose strength any one may test for themselves in a home hot-house,) or it might be some other tough intertwisted fibres or bush-twigs, pliant with young sap, such as those with which the traveller Roberts informs us he has seen the natives in India securing the wild elephant, and making a fetter strong enough to resist the strain of his enormous limbs. Never doubting of her success, she shouts aloud to the soldiers, whom Josephus speaks of as being 'hid in ambush within the house,'—"The Philistines be upon thee, Samson!" But ere they can reach the chamber, the giant had snapped the ligaments, "as a thread of tow is broken when it toucheth the fire." Delilah, thus baulked in her first attempt, returns to the charge; —again she whispers her blandishments in his facile ear, and makes a second earnest appeal to him to unlock the secret. Yet again he mocks her with a delusive reply;—for the new hempen ropes, which he suggests as his second device, are as unavailing to bind him as were the ropes of with: like tiny threads they are again snapped asunder. The third device is equally futile and delusive, but it has a dash, more than the others, about it of the pranks of the merry giant. In the rooms of ancient houses in the East where the women lived, there was almost invariably a distaff, the working of which formed the favourite employment of their leisure hours, as, indeed, was the case, in later times, with high-born ladies in England, not excluding those in the court of our sovereigns. In both cases, their recreation was to spin the thread afterwards employed in weaving fabrics on the loom. Even this latter, though of small dimensions, was no uncommon article of furniture in the apartments of the females in Palestine.

It seems to have been so in the case of Delilah. The eye of Samson falls on the wooden framework, with its beam and web and shuttle, and he humorously tells her to inweave his seven locks, rather than the hemp, and she will succeed in disarming his strength. She takes the earliest opportunity of making the experiment. Close by the loom she lulls him asleep, and when in this state of unconsciousness, she weaves, as he had suggested, the unshorn locks with the web. She seems this time, at all events, to have made sure of her victim. The old cry resounds, "The Philistines be upon thee, Samson!" More than ludicrous was the result. The strong lion who bore the strain of a city's gates on his shoulders, can now test the strength of his shaggy mane. He rises from his sleep—bearing away, apparently without effort, the cumbrous framework—and, doubtless, at the expense of the foiled enchantress, enjoying his own quiet or perhaps boisterous merriment.

The weakness of his nature comes out in the folly of longer dallying with the persistent temptress. But she has him within her toils, and he makes no effort, as he might easily have done, to evade certain ruin. She prepares for one other assault on the giant fortress—alas! with deadlier effect. She alternately chides and fondles. Day after day she returned to the entreaty, until his patience and good-nature were fairly overcome; for "she urged him so, that his soul was vexed unto death," (Judges xvi. 16.) As Milton graphically paraphrases it—

> "Mustering all her wiles
> With blandished parleys, feminine assaults,
> Tongue batteries—she surceased not, day nor night
> To storm me. Overwatched and wearied out,
> At times when men seek most repose and rest,
> I yielded, and unlocked her all my heart."

What was that unlocking? It was simply informing her of the facts with which we are so far already cognisant,—viz., that from his birth he had been a Nazarite, consecrated to the Great Being from whom he had derived his might; that the symbol of that consecration was his unshorn hair; that if she succeeded in depriving him of that, his superhuman power was at an end. She lost no time in communicating the revelation to the confederate chiefs. So certain were they now of the longed-for solution, that the money bribe—the recompense for her treachery—was brought along with them. Delilah chose mid-day, after the forenoon meal, (the *siesta*,) when her powerless victim would be heavy with sleep, for the accomplishment of her plot. Seating herself on a divan or raised couch, she would pillow the giant's head on her lap, and sing him asleep, at the same time sending for a barber to cut or shave off his seven locks. No sooner was the operation completed, than "his strength went from him." Uttering her former exclamation, "The Philistines be upon thee, Samson!"—the formidable hero, all unconscious at the moment of his loss, started up ready for action, saying, "I will go out as at other times before, and shake myself." But the strong muscle and athletic strength were powerless and gone—he had become weak as other men—invincible no more.

And now comes the final successful stroke of vengeance for a long series of humiliating depredations and insulting wrongs. The Philistines rush in upon their old enemy, and having secured his person, in order to prevent the possibility of escape or of fresh acts of spoliation, they resort to the barbarous custom—unfortunately so prevalent among ancient nations—of putting out the captive's eyes. There can be little doubt that his death was resolved on; and they would at once have despatched him with their daggers, had they not wished to gratify their wanton barbarity by taking him alive within the gates of their capital, and preceding death with insult. It is well known that nations boasting of greater civilization,—the Greeks and Romans, the Persians and Assyrians,—in the intoxication of victory, often stooped to the debasing expedient of dragging their vanquished foes in chains by their chariot wheels. We need not be astonished, therefore, that the Philistines resolved in the meantime to prolong Samson's life, in order that in some such way he might grace their savage triumph. By making cruel sport of him, they would illustrate and exemplify the old creed of fallen nature, "Thou shalt hate thine enemy." With all the hero's serious faults and vices, we confess to a deep sympathy with him in this his hour of fallen greatness, as we see the slayer of thousands—the mighty man of valour—groping his way in stone-blindness along the highway to Gaza—the butt of those who, a few days before, had trembled at the sound of his name.

> "Oh miserable change! is this the man,
> Renowned afar, the dread of Israel's foes,
> Who with an angel's strength their armies quelled—
> Himself an army." *

We find, at a later period of the Jewish history,

* Handel's *Samson*.

when Nebuchadnezzar, King of Babylon, came up with his hosts against Jerusalem, that the reigning sovereign of Judah, after a vain attempt at flight, was overtaken in the plains of Jericho; and not only were his eyes put out, but he was bound also with fetters of brass, and carried away to Babylon. It was the identical doom, in the present instance, of the Danite hero. On reaching Gaza, the Philistines were not content with having deprived him of his eyesight, but fetters of brass, similar to those with which Zedekiah was bound, were put upon him in exchange for his cords. Moreover, as if this indignity were insufficient, he was condemned, on being cast into prison, to grind the corn of his tormentors,—a species of punishment which was reserved only for women and slaves. When God is predicting, by the mouth of his prophet, the retribution that is to overtake the Chaldean captives of a future age, one of the marks of degradation specified is this: "Take the millstones and grind meal," (Isaiah xlvii. 2.) It was truly what is called in our penal code "punishment with hard labour;" and the hardest element in it to Samson's proud nature, would be the indignity to which, as a judge and a hero, it compelled him to stoop. We can, moreover, readily believe he was made the subject of many provocations and cruelties which are not specified in the narrative.

One arrow, more cruel than all, must have rankled in the once strong man's bosom—the arrow of self-reproach—that he had suffered himself to be duped and depraved by the artful slave of his own bad passions. Milton powerfully represents him as thus mourning his self-degradation and its bitter cause:—

"Foul effeminacy held me yoked,
Her bondslave. Oh indignity! Oh blot
To honour and religion! Servile mind,
Rewarded well with servile punishment!
The base degree to which I now am fallen—
These rags, this grinding—is not yet so base
As was my former servitude—ignoble,
Unmanly, ignominious, infamous,
True slavery, and that blindness worse than this
That saw not how degenerately I served."

And then follow the words, like a wild refrain or dirge—the same touching soliloquy which was repeated in his last hours of blindness and imbecility by England's aged king,—

"Oh dark, dark, dark! amid the blaze of noon
Irrecoverably dark! total eclipse,
Without all hope of day!"

But in malicious cruelty, one act of special and

crowning indignity is decreed. The five chiefs of the Philistines combine in resolving to hold a day of festal mirth at the expense of their captive. Like the thousands who assemble periodically at Bourgos and Madrid for the savage sport of bull-baiting, so is there to be a vast gathering at Gaza, to enjoy a similar barbarous pastime; only, on this occasion, the victim is to be a human one—the enemy of their country, the devastator of their fields, one, too, who had left not a few Philistine homes widowed and fatherless. To add to the impressiveness of the occasion, it is to be made a religious convocation. Samson has fallen—and his fall is to be attributed, in the eyes of his captors, to the great deity of their nation. The five Philistine lords issued a conjoint decree to all their people, to assemble together in order "to offer a great sacrifice unto Dagon their god, and to rejoice." As their only other deity, Baalzebub, "the lord of flies," had his sanctuary in Ekron, so Dagon, the "fish god," had his two principal temples at Gaza and Ashdod. Mr. Layard gives, among his other bas-reliefs from Nimroud, a representation of this idol. He is represented with the figure of a fish drooping behind from the crown of the head, while the god himself holds in one hand the sacred basket, and in the other the mystic fir-cone.

It would not appear that the Philistines held this national gathering within Dagon's temple. That was incapable of containing so vast a multitude. It is more probable that it would be in some building corresponding to a Roman amphitheatre, with raised seats and galleries to accommodate the spectators—the roof and galleries supported by two massive pillars in the centre of the structure. Very possibly an image of their deity would be introduced into some portion of the edifice, to lend a religious sanction to these wild and lawless revelries. The object on which all eyes would be turned was not the patron god, but the blind fallen hero. He is brought, like the baited animal of which we have spoken, into the midst of the arena. The pride of Philistia—its lords, and princes, and warriors, including, doubtless, its high-born women and damsels—all the beauty and chivalry of the kingdom—have gathered together to witness the sport. Upon the roof alone there were 3000 men and women. A wild shout would go up from the assemblage as he was led in, or groped his way with his eyeless sockets. "When the people saw him, they praised their god: for they said, Our god hath delivered into our hands our enemy, and the destroyer of our country, which slew many of us," (xiv. 24.) But they were not content with a mere sight of the degraded man. They had at first, probably, called him in, while the sacrifice was being offered to Dagon. But, in accordance with the invariable practice after the completion of the sacrificial rite, follows the feast, at which they seem to have worked themselves into a state of boisterous excitement. Samson, we gather from the narrative, had been for a little remanded to his prison; but another more savage demand and cry is heard to bring him forth again, not merely to see him, but that he may be made to act the part of jester or buffoon, and minister to their merriment,—"Call for Samson, that he may make us sport." The natural playfulness of his nature seems irrepressible even in this hour of humiliation. We could have wished it had been otherwise. More truly noble in every way would have been the tragical close of his story, if, with the stern dignity of the Judge, and proud submission of the vanquished hero, he had refused the ignominious task of gratifying their sense of the ludicrous, even though they had threatened compulsion with the lash and torture. But the impression left upon us is, that he stooped to gratify their demand, and by every strange and wild prank and gambol of his buoyant days convulsed the spectators with laughter. That savage merriment, and these orgies, however, were soon to give place to a wild wail of anguish. By one of those strange, sudden transitions from mirth to soberness, from puerile imbecility to manly dignity and strength, not uncommon in some characters, the fallen hero seems all at once to have risen to the consciousness of his position as the servant and representative of Jehovah. Possibly confronting the dumb idol of the heathen oppressors, he is resolved, in a strength greater than his own, to vindicate the insulted honour of Israel's God before that jeering mob. The old symbol of his former strength was beginning to reappear—"the hair of his head began to grow again." With it returned his giant strength. The very scoffs and buffetings that rise around him would doubtless prove incentives to the putting forth of that restored might in one grand final testimony to the supremacy of Jehovah. He knows, perhaps, too well, that these bacchanal revelries will end in his being put to death. Can he not anticipate the murderers, and, by one gigantic effort, bury them and himself in the ruins of the building where they were assembled?

The blind champion asks the young slave who leads him by the hand to conduct him to the two central pillars. He does so. The countless eyes upon him can see nothing but the baited, buffeted hero, leaning for weariness and exhaustion after hours of savage play. But, unknown to them, in the midst of the noise and hubbub, from those giant lips and that fretted spirit there is ascending words of prayer to the God he served: —"O Lord God, remember me, I pray thee, and strengthen me, I pray thee, only this once, O God," (xvi. 28.)

"See, he comes, with fettered tread,
Bursting heart and drooping head;
Flowing tresses, quickly grown,
O'er his shoulders wildly thrown;
Arms with superhuman power,
Nerved for that momentous hour.

Shouts of savage joy arise,
While, with fixed and wondering eyes,
On this peerless man they gaze,
All absorbed in strange amaze.
But they know not, God is there,
Hearing, owning, answering prayer."

And yet, once more, as it has been well noted, his "grim playfulness is strong in death." He asks to be led to the *two* pillars, that he may be avenged of the Philistines for his *two* eyes—(a pillar for each eye.) His last prayer was that he himself might not survive the crash, for he well knew it would only be to undergo more aggravated torture. "He bowed himself with all his might," and grasping a pillar in each hand, the vast edifice rocks to its foundation. In another moment it is a heap of mangled flesh and bones—dead and dying,—the giant himself lies at the bottom of the mass, amid the crowd of victims. And so, "the life which began in marvel ends in deepest tragedy," (Milman.) Here, again, we may note that the feat of Samson would appear to have suggested the similar deed of vengeance attributed to the Pagan Hercules, and would seem to confirm the supposition, that the stalwart Hebrew of Palestine was the original of the later creation of the Western nations. Herodotus tells us that "Hercules once went to Egypt, and there the inhabitants took him, and putting a chaplet on his head, led him out in solemn procession, intending to offer him as a sacrifice to Jupiter. For a while he submitted quietly; but when they led him up to the altar, and began the ceremonies, he put forth his strength, and slew them all."

Milton's rendering of the scene at Gaza, may here be given:—

> "With horrible convulsion to and fro
> He tugged, he shook; till down they came, and drew
> The whole roof after them, with burst of thunder,
> Upon the heads of all who sat beneath,—
> Lords, ladies, captains, councillors, and priests,—
> Their choice nobility and flower, not only
> Of this, but each Philistine city round,
> Met from all parts to solemnize the feast.
> Samson, with these, inmixt, inevitably
> Pulled down the same destruction on himself."

The sacred narrative closes with the simple but touching account of the great victim's burial. His mourning father and all his clan came down to fetch the dead body. The Philistines, though they had insulted him in his last moments, perhaps, by the terrible closing catastrophe, dreaded what further vengeance might overtake them by insulting his ashes. They were, perhaps, glad of their removal. We can fancy in thought the mournful cortege giving utterance to wild laments and dirges for the illustrious dead, as it ascended amid the vineyards which had witnessed his early exploits, up to his mountain home, finally consigning his disfigured frame to the cave "of Manoah his father."

> "Come, come: no time for lamentation now,
> No cause for grief, Samson like Samson fell,
> Both life and death heroic. To his foes
> Ruin is left; to him, eternal fame."—*Handel.*

This great master of sacred song, who has so powerfully embodied the events of the champion's life in his well-known *Oratorio*—has, with equal poetic beauty and power, represented the solemn gathering around the family sepulchre. The finest portion, perhaps, of his great work, are the lines and music introduced in this closing scene. One of Samson's friends who has been standing by his grave among the crowd of mourners, celebrates his deeds, and mourns his departure. As he concludes with lauding him for having filled Philistia's land with desolation, and

> "Honour and freedom giv'n to Jacob's seed,"

a damsel of Israel—no "hired minstrel,"—thus calls for louder strains than earth can afford, to celebrate the hero's praise—

> "Let the bright seraphim in burning row
> Their loud uplifted angel trumpets blow;
> Let the cherubic host, in tuneful choirs
> Touch their immortal harp with golden wires."

I have referred to more than one incident in the

history of this Warrior-Judge which seems strikingly to correspond to similar feats in the life of the fabled Hercules of Roman and Greek mythology. I cannot better close than with the following picture a writer gives of the Pagan hero, bearing, as it does, so remarkable a resemblance to Samson:—"Hercules was a jovial guest, and not backward in enjoying himself. . . . It was he, above all heroes, whom mythology placed in ludicrous situations, and sometimes made the butt of the buffoonery of others. . . . The highest degree of human suffering and courage is attributed to Hercules; his character is as noble as could be conceived in these rude and early ages; but he is by no means represented as free from the blemishes of human nature; on the contrary, he is frequently subject to wild, ungovernable passions, when the noble indignation and anger of the suffering hero degenerate into frenzy. Every crime, however, is atoned for by some new suffering; but nothing breaks his invincible courage," (*Art.* "*Samson*," Smith's *Bible Dictionary.*)

Samson's frequent and successful conflicts with the Philistines, and especially his last and concluding destruction of them in presence of their national deity, was intended as a great lesson and parable to Israel and the Church—indeed to individuals in all ages—that if only true to the service and will of God, like him, out of weakness they will be made strong, wax valiant in fight, and turn to flight the armies of the aliens. In concluding this brief account of him and of the other Warrior-Judges of Israel, we cannot resist, amid the tales of cruelty and oppression, of murder, and massacre, and wrong, to long for that better day, and the coming of that better "Warrior-Judge," who is to go forth on the "white horse" of victory, with the bow of peaceful conquest in his hand, "conquering and to conquer;"—who is to usher in the predicted era when "Judah and Israel"—aye, the whole earth—"shall dwell safely, every man under his vine and fig-tree." Alas! it is as true in our own days as in those of Hebrew history, that "the battle of the warrior is with confused noise, and garments rolled in blood." But the period is nearing (may God speed it!) when the reign of the Prince of Peace will terminate and supersede all warrior tales—when "He shall JUDGE among the nations, and shall rebuke many people: and they shall beat their swords into ploughshares, and their spears into pruning-hooks; nation shall not lift up sword against nation; neither shall they learn war any more," (Isaiah ii. 4.)

We cannot more appropriately conclude, than with the sublime closing prayer with which we are now familiar from the song of Deborah:—

> "So let all thine enemies perish, O Lord!
> But let them that love thee be as the sun,
> When he goeth forth in his might."